The Resonance of My Thoughts

Francis Nii

2nd Edition
Copyright © 2017 Francis Nii
francisnii23@gmail.com
All rights reserved.
ISBN-10: 1979425299
ISBN-13: 978-1979425292
Cover photograph by Jimmy Awagl

DEDICATION

Dedicated to all the bookworms, especially grade 10-12 students throughout Papua New Guinea and to Ambo Nii and Yannie John Konia and the troops at Wara Simbu.

.

CONTENTS

ACKNOWLEDGMENTS

All the articles in this volume have been edited and published by Professor Keith Jackson on his blog *PNG Attitude.*

Keith was once a teacher at Gon Primary School in the Simbu Province in the 1960s. Currently he is the Chairman of Jacksons PR based in Queensland and Publisher and Administrator of the *PNG Attitude* blog. He is the co-founder of Crocodile Prize, an annual national literature competition in PNG.

Thanks to Philip Fitzpatrick for the final eye and uploading the manuscript onto Create-Space under Pukpuk Publishing. Phil was once a kiap in what is now known as Western Province during the colonial administration of the Territory. Currently he is an anthropologist, consultant and author of many books and is based in Queensland. He is also the co-founder of Crocodile Prize.

Gratitude also to all the doctors and nurses of Sir Joseph Nombri Memorial Hospital Kundiawa, especially Dr Jaworski and Dr Urakoko (the team leaders) and the staff of Jaworski Wing Two for giving me special privileges to carry on with my writing whilst living in the ward.

1

Machiavellian Moments 2011-12 : 1 - Seizure of the Executive Power

APART from the 1988-1997 Bougainville conflict, Peter O'Neill's takeover of executive power from Grand Chief Sir Michael Somare and the consequent political impasse of 2011-2012 marked one of the most turbulent and perilous periods in the political history of Papua New Guinea.

It was four years ago that then prime minister Somare left PNG for Singapore's Raffles Hospital to receive treatment for a heart condition. He was to be there for over five months.

Before he left for Singapore, Somare elevated foreign affairs minister Sam Abal, son of independence politician Sir Tei Abal, to be acting prime minister, overlooking deputy prime minister Don Polye.

At the time, Peter O'Neill was Minister for Works.

On 28 June 2011, Arthur Somare, son of Sir Michael and MP for Angoram, announced on behalf of the Somare family that his father had stepped down from politics for health reasons.

There was media speculation at the time about the physical and mental fitness of Somare and whether he was capable of performing the duties of prime minister.

On 2 August 2011, Speaker Jeffrey Nape declared the prime minister's seat vacant and Peter O'Neill was subsequently appointed Prime Minister and Belden Namah his deputy under section 142(2) of the Constitution.

Peter Charles Paire O'Neill CMG, the son of Australian kiap Brian O'Neill and Awambo Yari from Pangia in the Southern Highlands Province, was appointed the eighth prime minister of PNG 70-24 in a parliamentary vote.

O'Neill was educated at Pangia Primary School, Ialibu High School and Aiyura National High School. In 1986, he graduated from University of Papua New Guinea with a bachelor of accountancy and commerce.

O'Neill was a businessman before entering politics at the 2002 general election, in which he had ousted the incumbent member for Ialibu-Pangia and veteran politician, Roy Yaki. He retained the seat at the 2007 general elections and easily retained the seat in 2012.

One of the power players in the dethroning of Somare and Abal was Vanimo Green MP Belden Namah, a logging tycoon and former PNG Defence Force officer.

Namah was instrumental in toppling the Somare regime and installing Peter O'Neill as prime minister. He rewarded himself with the deputy's role and the forestry and climate change portfolio.

The change of government occurred amidst a backdrop of high profile shady dealing including the Julian Moti affair, the $30 million Taiwan diplomacy scandal and the Indonesian fugitive Djoko Tjandra (aka Joe Chan) affair.

At the time, most sectors of the community applauded the power swap. Even the churches flapped their wings and said it was God's answer to their prayers for change.

But the East Sepik provincial government continued to support Somare and challenged O'Neill's appointment before the Supreme Court under section 19 of the Constitution.

The key point of argument was whether there was a vacancy in the prime minister's seat at the time of O'Neill's election.

On 18 August 2011, the O'Neill-led Cabinet [national executive council] retaliated by suspending the financial powers of the provincial government, threatening to suspend it if it didn't withdraw its court action.

But East Sepik Governor Peter Wararu-Waranaka and his provincial executive council did not flinch. Wararu stated that only Parliament could suspend the provincial government.

He said the national executive council had no power to take such action and refused to meet with the inter-government relations minister Mark Maipakai and the NEC when each separately summonsed him in writing to meet with them.

Somare maintained there was no vacancy and said he was ready and able to complete his term as the only legally elected prime minister.

In September 2011, he circulated a signed statement to the media, his first since he had been admitted to Raffles Hospital in April. It said: "Sections 142-145 of the Papua New Guinea Constitution is very clear about the election and removal of a prime minister. There has never been a vacancy in the position of prime minister.

"As elected representatives we must uphold the Constitution of Papua New Guinea and respect the independent role of the Supreme Court and, therefore, not pre-empt any judgment. O'Neill should know that East Sepik provincial government is fully acting within its right to file a Supreme Court reference under section 19 of the Constitution by questioning the legitimacy of the election.

"If O'Neill thinks that his election is legitimate, he should not feel threatened by the actions of the East Sepik provincial government. The Supreme Court reference raises legitimate questions and has a right to be heard."

On 6 September, the member for Sinasina-Yongomugl and Speaker of national parliament Jeffrey Nape used his discretion to dismiss Sir Michael from parliament for purportedly having missed three consecutive sessions.

The dismissal notice said in part: "It is my solemn duty to advise you that by operation of section 104(2) (d) of the Constitution, your former seat, East Sepik Provincial, is now vacant.

"According to the attendance records [and minutes] of parliament, you were absent during the whole of three consecutive sittings of parliament since February 2011 without leave of parliament for such an absence. In these circumstances the constitution operates to automatically cause your seat to be vacant.

"I note that … parliament granted you leave of absence for the duration of that meeting only. Regrettably the motion of the 17 May 2011 was defective and ineffective to avert the operation of Section 104(2) (d) of the Constitution because the only leave of absence contemplated by that Section is a leave of absence for three consecutive meetings.

"For reasons best known to your advisors, no such leave was sought, and no such leave was granted. The motion of 17 May 2011 operated in respect of only one meeting of the parliament."

Nape's action was in direct contradiction to clerk of

parliament Don Pandan's earlier advice that Somare had missed only two sittings and his presence would avoid any termination.

"I confirm that my records constituting the minutes of proceedings of parliament as required by Standing Orders 30 for 2011 show that Sir Michael has been absent for only the June and August meetings of parliament," Pandan advised.

"I confirm that when Sir Michael attends today's meeting of parliament, he will avoid being absent for three consecutive meetings of parliament and thus being disqualified as the Member for East Sepik regional seat, pursuant to the requirements of Section 104(2)(d) of the Constitution."

In defiance of Pandan's advice, Parliament voted on the voices to accept the Speaker's decision.

On 26 October 2011, the Supreme Court in Waigani dismissed an application by the O'Neill-Namah government to stop the Constitutional reference. The move was made by Dr Allan Marat, Attorney-General in the O'Neill government and had the support of the Speaker Jeffrey Nape, O'Neill and Namah.

It was argued that the decision to seek Supreme Court reference by the East Sepik provincial government did not carry the endorsement of the full provincial executive council members. Only 12 out of the 15 Provincial Executive Council members had attended the meeting that passed the resolution for the reference.

The Supreme Court however ruled in favour of the East Sepik provincial government that there was a quorum and the PEC meeting was in order. The decision paved the way for the reference to be heard.

The Court also warned the O'Neill government to refrain from issuing threats against the East Sepik provincial government.

On 12 December 2011, the crisis reached climax when a full bench Supreme Court sitting headed by Chief Justice Sir Salamo

Injia ruled 3-2 that the election of O'Neill was unconstitutional and ordered the reinstatement of Somare.

The court ruled that the office of the prime minister was not vacant, hence the election of O'Neill and Namah was unconstitutional and unlawful.

The Supreme Court decision put the office of the Governor-General in a dilemma about whether to recognise the minority (19 MPs) Supreme Court reinstated prime minister Somare or the overwhelming (50 MPs) parliamentary supported prime minister O'Neill.

Legally Sir Michael Ogio had no choice but to comply with the Supreme Court's decision. So on 14 December 2011, Ogio installed Somare as the legitimate prime minister of Papua New Guinea.

A few hours after Somare's swearing in, the O'Neill government, through a motion on the floor of parliament chaired by O'Neill himself, suspended Ogio and, by law, Speaker Nape automatically became acting governor-general.

In his capacity as acting governor-general, Nape proceeded to swear in O'Neill as prime minister.

However, Queen Elizabeth II, the titular head of PNG who appoints the governor-general on the advice of the prime minister, had not revoked vice-regal Ogio's commission.

On 16 December, O'Neill announced that he had the support of state institutions. Indeed, the public service, military, police and correctional service backed him and were taking directions from the O'Neill-Namah government.

On 19 December, parliament lifted Ogio's suspension as governor-general after he admitted his recognition of Somare as prime minister was based on flawed advice. The next day, Ogio recognised O'Neill as prime minister.

"With the Governor-General now following the head of the public service and police chief in recognising Peter O'Neill as prime minister," journalist Johnny Blades of Radio New Zealand International reported, "[Somare] appears to have lost most of his significant support bases.

"Sir Michael is refusing to back down from his claim to be the Prime Minister and insists that the constitution he helped write as PNG gained independence in 1975 must rule supreme.

"However with Sir Michael barely seen in public since impasse began, Peter O'Neill has been confidently asserting control of the public institutions. He described the Governor-general's confirmation of his Prime Ministership as the perfect Christmas present for the nation."

Many of those people who had avidly followed the saga would have agreed with the Supreme Court decision that the appointment of O'Neill and Namah was unconstitutional and would also agree that the affair was riddled with unprincipled and crafty strategies which were evil in nature and not of God.

Had Grand Chief Somare conceded defeat? We'll find out in the next episode.

2

Machiavellian Moments 2011-12: 2 – Mutiny, Prequel and Sequel

FINDING the going against the O'Neill-Namah axis getting tougher, Sir Michael Somare reportedly requested then PNG Defence Force Commander, Brigadier-General Francis Angwi, for a military intervention to restore him to power.

Angwi, a Sepik like Somare, had been appointed Commander by the Somare government but he refused the invitation and instead turned to Peter O'Neill as the legitimate prime minister. The police and the correctional services also sided with O'Neill-Namah.

Somare and his cabinet in a never-say-die determination to regain the throne then appointed retired Colonel Yaura Sasa from Morobe Province as PNGDF Commander to replace Angwi.

The appointment was done in stealth and kept secret. There was no official announcement and the public did not know about it until 3 am on 26 January 2012 when Colonel Sasa and soldiers loyal to Somare detained Angwi and two other officers loyal to O'Neill.

It is recorded that 20 soldiers from the 1st Battalion, Royal Pacific Island Regiment detained Angwi and the two other officers after overpowering guards at Taurama Barracks.

Several shots were fired and the mutineers transported Angwi to Murray Barracks where he was placed under house arrest.

At a press conference held later the same day, Sasa claimed his actions were not mutiny as he had been appointed to lead the PNGDF by Somare. Sasa called upon Governor-General Sir Michael Ogio to reinstate the Grand Chief and asked all parties to respect the Constitution and comply with the orders issued by the Supreme Court.

Namah, in a separate press conference, stated that Sasa was not supported by most PNGDF soldiers, and that 15 of his supporters had been arrested. The total number of military personnel supporting the Colonel was said to be about 30.

Namah claimed that Sasa's actions constituted treason and sought his surrender.

On 28 January police arrested Sasa at Boroko and charged him with mutiny and, two days later, the soldiers who participated in the mutiny surrendered their weapons to Namah following a parade at Taurama Barracks.

Namah gave a speech to 200 members of the 1st Battalion stating that the mutineers would receive an amnesty and that any personnel who participated in any further mutinies would face the "full brunt of the law".

Sasa was released on bail on 1 February. Six months later, on 1 August 2012, the charge against Sasa was struck out by a committal court on the grounds that police prosecutors had not submitted evidence to substantiate the charges.

After the dissolution of the mutiny, Somare was effectively impotent. He was no longer a threat to O'Neill and Namah.

On 18 March, the O'Neill-led parliament counteracted the Supreme Court's ruling that O'Neill's appointment as prime minister was illegal. It also passed the controversial Judicial Conduct Act 2012. O'Neill-Namah saw the Judiciary as their new threat after effectively emasculating Somare.

The Judicial Conduct Act gave parliament powers to suspend senior judges who, in the eyes of the government, were deemed to be biased in their decisions. This raised serious issues of the separation of powers between judiciary and legislature and of the independence of the judiciary.

The enforcement of the Act was in retrospective to 1 November 2011 which effectively voided all of the critical court decisions impugning the legitimacy of the O'Neill-Namah regime.

Among the affected decisions were the Supreme Court orders of December 12 which reinstated Somare to the post of prime minister, the contempt of court action against Namah, Attorney General Allan Marat and other leaders, and other consequential orders.

It was widely seen that the Act was clearly designed to denigrate the powers of the judiciary and was not healthy for PNG's democracy.

Of those who openly opposed the Act were Moresby South MP and opposition leader Dame Carol Kidu, the Community Coalition Against Corruption, the PNG Trade Union Congress, Transparency International PNG and students from the University of PNG.

Dame Carol, the only opposition MP who was allowed to debate the Act on the floor of parliament, fervently argued that the law would erode the separation of powers between executive and judiciary.

The preamble to a petition signed by 1,086 UPNG students and presented to chief of staff Manasupe Zurenouc on 23 March read in part:

"As educated Papua New Guineans we have discussed the Bill at length in forums sanctioned by the UPNG SRC. We have had our Law students, Politics students, Public Policy students and students from all schools of thought read into the bill and offer their learned views on what this law effectively means for the future of Governance in Papua New Guinea.

"And we have, in one voice concluded that the Judicial Conduct Bill is dangerous and abusive of established Constitutional and legislative processes and Offices already in operation."

"Parliament is fallible and not beyond reproach" and asked; "if the judiciary is now answerable to parliament then who is parliament answerable to?" Transparency International asked.

On 10 April 2012, addressing more than 1,000 protesters demanding for the repeal of the Act, Peter O'Neill stated that its repeal was conditional on the stepping down of chief justice Sir Salamo Injia and justice Nicholas Kiriwom.

It was now clear that the underlying spirit of the Judicial Conduct Act was to avenge Injia and Kiriwom for their decisions.

But the leaders of the protesters refused to accept any conditions and were resolute in their demand that the Act be repealed without any strings attached. On 5 January 2013, the Judicial Conduct Act was repealed by Parliament due to wide spread dissents and protests.

Many people who followed these events even to this day would feel that Somare had set the stage for his own downfall before he went to Singapore when he appointed Sam Abal as acting prime minister overlooking the incumbent deputy Don Polye. But in reality this was just the igniting factor.

The seed for the saga was sown earlier when in 2010 the National Court ruled that specific provisions in the Organic Law on the Integrity of Political Parties and Candidates (OLIPAC) that assured the continuity of a prime minister in office breached individual members freedom of choice and were rendered null and void.

This was thoroughly explained by Professor Henry Okole in a commentary, *It's time for Somare and O'Neill to end political stalemate*. [*Papua New Guinea issues in Perspective*, 17 January 2012]

"The National Alliance's protective cover was blown wide open when specific provisions in that law [OLIPAC] that assured the continuity of a prime minister were rendered null and void", Professor Okole noted.

"The Supreme Court ruling was what finally unscrewed the bolts of a period that many people regard as a period of 'stability' under the OLIPAC.

"In the haste to stabilize parliamentary politics, the OLIPAC guaranteed a prime minister to serve out a full five year term while the option to invoke a vote of no confidence was technically shunned.

"In that regard the inability to change the Somare government through a vote of no confidence did not create stability; rather it created animosity.

"No doubt Somare's hospitalisation … as many people would argue – did precipitate the domino effect that culminated in everything that has happened and ended with the current stalemate. People can talk about the divisive issues in the National Alliance, the acting role of Sam Abal as prime minister and the medical condition of Chief Somare, among many things.

"But the seeds of destruction were sowed well before the Chief entered hospital. The change of government on 2 August 2011 was not only a change of prime minister and government. To some MPs, it was to avenge themselves - after feeling victimized and betrayed - against certain colleagues of theirs who plied their alleged dirty trade behind Chief Somare.

"In a way, the public support for the O'Neill-Nama government was a reaction also to some of these leaders who saw themselves as being indispensable to PNG politics."

Somare ignited the bomb with his appointment of Abal as the acting prime minister instead of Polye. Polye was the National Alliance parliamentary deputy leader for the Highlands region and deputy prime minister.

The most principled, rational and wisest thing for Somare to do was to appoint Polye as acting prime minister. He was one of the most senior members of parliament and more than qualified to be acting prime minister.

Had Somare appointed Polye, the government would have been placed in respectable and capable hands and have remained intact until Somare returned from Singapore.

Why did Somare overlook Polye and appoint Abal?

In my view, it was because of the uncertainty pertaining to Somare's future due to his deteriorating health. Somare was attempting to pave the way for his son Arthur to succeed him as prime minister. This would not be feasible if the acting post was granted to Polye who was well set to become prime minister. Arthur would find it difficult to take the reins from him.

Somare reckoned it would be easy for Arthur to take power from Abal hence he bestowed the acting position on the least likely contender.

This blunder triggered disappointment and dissent among the Highlands National Alliance bloc headed by Polye and the disintegration of National Alliance Party which made much easier the overthrow of the Somare dynasty.

3

Machiavellian Moments: 3 – A Dissertation on Truth & Innocence

ON 2 January 2013, seven months after the political stalemate and the general elections, Somare and his National Alliance Party buried the hatchet and married Peter O'Neill's National Congress Party in Alotau and made O'Neill the ninth Prime Minister.

Given that Somare's personal reputation, clout and dominance had been tarnished, humiliated, dragged and muddied by O'Neill and his cohorts, the Grand Chief's surprising volte-face prominently overshadowed all the outstanding constitutional references, court proceedings and other outstanding issues and paved the way for normalcy and stability.

The impasse and its related events were water under the bridge. Consigned to history were the ousting of the Grand Chief from Parliament and his East Sepik provincial seat (subsequently regained at the general election), the military fracas, the enactment of the controversial judicial conduct laws, and the storming of the National Court by Belden Namah in pursuit of the Chief Justice, Sir Salamo Injia.

It seemed that O'Neill was now on a stable turf until Investigative Task Force Sweep, the corruption busting agency of the state which he, Peter O'Neill, was instrumental in establishing in August 2011, began to undertake some serious work.

It had been established just ten days after O'Neill seized power from Somare and began an investigation into allegations of corruption at the Department of Planning and Monitoring. The sleuthing implicated O'Neill in a multimillion corrupt deal now popularly known as Parakagate.

O'Neill has resolutely defended himself against the allegation since the matter surfaced in a massive investigation into the Finance Department turning up one of Task Force Sweep's key pieces of evidence.

It was an authorisation letter containing the prime minister's signature which O'Neill said was forged. It was sent off for forensic testing which affirmed the signature was O'Neill's and not a forgery.

But O'Neill was adamant that the signature on the letter of 24 June 2012 authorizing the payment of K71.8 million of state money to Paul Paraka is not his. He claims that someone else signed the letter.

Then, in the face of a potential arrest, he accused Task Force Sweep, police and even the judiciary of collusion and politicization and alluded to a plot to overthrow him. There was never any evidence of a plot, and to my mind, on the basis of the forensic test result, O'Neill did not tell the truth about the signature.

There is a credible indication that the signature on the authorisation letter belongs to O'Neill and that he himself signed the letter.

If O'Neill thought the forensic test was biased or flawed because of collusion between Task Force Sweep, police investigators and the forensic tester then, the rational thing to do was to seek independent forensic tests.

How else could he prove that he didn't sign the letter that associated with the corrupt transfer of funds?

Furthermore, if O'Neill done no wrong, the simplest and most honourable action for him to take was to present himself to the police investigators, answering their queries and clearing his good name.

By doing so, he would also live by what has always preached: that no citizen, no matter how powerful, is above the law. This straightforward action would have not only maintained his integrity but also upheld the dignity of his office.

But instead, he has refused to engage with the police investigators and taken to court to block and prevent normal police operations to uphold the law and ensure the administration of justice. This avoidance action casts doubt over his claim of innocence and incorruptibility.

If O'Neill has done no wrong, there was no reason for him to fear the former Deputy Police Commissioner Operations Simon Kaupa, former Attorney General Kerenga Kua, Task Force Sweep head Sam Koim (still superintending a disbanded organisation) and others who took a stand against corruption and seek justice.

Instead he has incapacitated them by termination and disbandment. His actions appear to me to indicate fear and desperation to conceal something and avoid the processes of justice.

Even if the court clears O'Neill of any wrongdoing, I will never be convinced that he has not played a role in the siphoning millions of kina to Paraka Lawyers that rightly belong to the 7.5 million people of PNG.

Truth will always remain the truth. One can deny the truth but it cannot be changed.

A man, any man, who is innocent in a free society, does not fear and run from the law. Only one who breaks the law fears, runs and hides from it. But the running cannot last forever. One day the long arm of the law will find our man and justice will prevail.

4

Is Changing the Government a Solution to Corruption in PNG?

IN the last couple of months, there have been deep sentiments for the change of government by political lobbyists and critics, especially in the social media.

The underlying raison d'être is discontent about some of the decisions made by the government. Among a number of decisions alleged to have involved corruption of some sort are the amendments to the Vote of No Confidence Act, the government's takeover of the PNG Sustainable Development Program and the Ok Tedi Mine, the asylum seekers deal with Australia, the awarding of medical kit supply contract to Borneo Pacific Pharmaceuticals and more recently the Parakagate.

Bloggers and users of social media are the prominent advocates of this discourse. Some even joined hands with the PNG Opposition in strategizing to topple the government. A case in point was the call for a nationwide strike on the eve of the budget session last November that went amiss.

Advocating for change in leadership is a typical Papua New Guinean way of reacting to unpopular policies and allegations of corruption by successive governments and there is nothing wrong with that.

Dr Martin Luther King Jr. once said in his civil rights campaign: "The moment you become silent about the things that matter, you are dead". Citizens have the moral obligation to raise concerns about government decisions that they feel are not in the best interest of their country.

However, the critical question is this: is changing government a solution to corruption? In other words, will the change of government have any tangible impact on corruption?

Corruption has been the main platform for the changes of government on the floor of parliament through votes of no confidence in the past.

The ousting of Grand Chief Sir Michael Somare by Pius Wingti in March 1980, Wingti by Sir Rabbie Namaliu in 1988, and Wingti by Sir Julius Chan in August 1994 and the dismantling of Somare's National Alliance regime by O'Neill and Nama in 2011 were all directly or indirectly motivated by anticorruption notions.

But has corruption changed? No. Corruption still exists and has become systemic and complicated. It has become a national plague. Why?

The answers lie in our political culture from the way elections are conducted, the way governments are formed and the modus operandi of governance. These peak political activities are mostly flawed.

The election system is the breeding ground of corruption. Trading cash and cargo for votes has become deeply rooted. A candidate who is serious about winning an election has to spend a lot of money and provide a lot of cargo to bribe as many voters as possible to muster the winning numbers.

Nere-tere … eat and give is a well-known election catchphrase in Simbu.

Consequently, when the new member gets elected to parliament, the first thing on his mind is to recoup what he has spent. That's when all kinds of vices creep in.

Often these people lack leadership qualities. They are prone to vice, negligence, mismanagement and dishonesty because they enter parliament by wicked ways.

The golden handshake is a rite of welcoming MPs to one's side during the formation of government. Venality is a well-grounded tradition during this horse trading.

Leadership ethics in PNG must be amongst the poorest in the world. There is no moral conscience in most of our leaders.

Politicians can be accused of serious corruption and they will still cling to office. They will appear in public if as nothing is wrong with them. They don't feel ashamed. They don't have a guilty conscience.

They will even go to court seeking vindication for their wrong doing. It is very unethical and shameful but this is PNG.

In most societies we don't see this kind of leadership. The moment a politician is accused of a scandal in the public media, he or she steps down immediately and paves the way for independent investigation. Or he or she resigns from holding public office if personal reputation is brought into disrepute.

In Papua New Guinea not one politician has resigned from ministerial portfolio or public office on the basis of moral principle.

Moreover, the culture of nepotism in the allocation of project funds and disbursement of District services improvement moneys make good leaders become yoyos. They compromise their ethics to align with the government of the day.

Tobias Kulang, the member for Kundiawa-Gembogl, is a professed Christian and a strong advocate against corruption. He had been vocal against the O'Neill government on many fronts and yet he crossed the floor and joined government ranks citing the interests of his electorate as his reason and he was right. If he remained in the Opposition his District would miss out on projects and DSIP funds.

Although he was a good leader, the flawed and crafty system of governance dictated his crossing of sides at the cost of his reputation.

Of course there are some good leaders but the system of governance is so flawed that it is like a cobweb that has been firmly entrenched and will continue to snare and smear them no matter who becomes the prime minister.

Task Force Sweep was the only corruption busting agency that did some real and intrepid work in the fight against corruption by uncovering and prosecuting some high profile corruption cases like the Paul Tiensten, Eremas Wartoto and the Parakagate cases to name a few.

But the problem was that TFS was not a constitutional office. It was only an ad hoc office established through a parliamentary decision and was subject to the whip of the government of the day as it has been experienced when O'Neill disbanded it in relation to the Parakagate.

Drastic reformation of the political culture from electioneering process to formation of government and subsequent active governance will need changes in attitudes to corruption.

The biometric electioneering system, tightening of the loopholes in the political party integrity law and the establishment of Independent Commission Against Corruption (ICAC) in place of TFS are positive reforms that need to be fast tracked.

Moreover, if PNG is serious about rooting out corruption at the leadership level, a very drastic reform in the leadership code is needed.

The current law regarding the onus of proof that says an accused is innocent until proven guilty in the court of law should change under the leadership code. In that, when any leader be it politicians, departmental heads, CEOs of government agencies and state owned enterprises are implicated or accused of a corruption, automatically they should be held in custody as guilty and the onus should be on them to prove their innocence in the court of law.

And if the court upholds the guilty status then a minimum of 25 years imprisonment should be the penalty regardless of the seriousness of the crime as long as it is corruption in nature.

If this country doesn't take such a tough approach and continue to be lenient and wishy-washy, politicians and the those who are in position of authority will continue to bend rules or manipulate the system to siphon and get rich while the poor will continue to be poor and cry over spilt morsels.

In conclusion, changing one corrupt government with another corrupt government will take us to nowhere in the fight against corruption. Drastic reform is the way forward.

5

Simbu's Successful Creative Approach to Service Delivery

THE efficacy of government services delivery in PNG is a continuing vexatious issue.

In a country of difficult geography, resources disparity, diverse cultures and lopsided infrastructure, the delivery of government services like transport, education and basic health care will continue to be a challenge for many years to come.

This problem of service delivery is well summed-up in *Why we give aid to PNG?*, an article published by the Australian Department of Foreign Affairs and Trade.

"Delivering Aid in PNG poses enormous challenges," it says.

"Providing basic services to very small, diverse, scattered and often isolated communities across extremely rugged terrain is a difficult task.

"Difficulties in reaching rural locations, weak governance and a lack of commitment to improving service delivery means many people still lack access to basic services such as education, transport and primary health care."

Amidst these challenges, Simbu Province has managed to out-perform the other 21 provinces in service delivery for three consecutive years.

The National Economic and Fiscal Commission ranked Simbu as performing better in the delivery of services to her people in 2011, 2012 and 2013.

So what is Simbu's secret for this consistent out-performance?

The province is located in the central highlands of PNG and has a land area of about 6,000 square kilometres. It is one of the densely populated provinces, the 2011 national census reporting 376,000 people with a population density of 62 a square kilometre.

Simbu's terrain is extremely rugged and undulating - full of mountains, steep canyons and fast flowing rivers.

Economically, Simbu is one of the poorest provinces. Apart from smallholder coffee plots of 1-2 hectares scattered down the sides of precipitous hills, there is no major economic resource base such as is found in other provinces.

There was much talk early this year about a Chinese company wanting to mine the province's abundant limestone, however that talk seemed to evaporate into the thin Simbu air.

If the project ever happens, it will be the first large-scale revenue earner for the province. Otherwise Simbu will remain poor.

In terms of transport infrastructure, most districts of Simbu are connected by road except Karimui where you need to take a plane.

The upgrading and sealing of trunk roads namely the Kundiawa-Gumine and Chuave-Siane (completed) and Kundiawa-Gembogl (in progress) have to some extent facilitated service delivery.

Otherwise many hamlets are scattered in isolated and remote areas and have no direct road links.

Added to these obstacles are the frequent landslips along the Highlands Highway between the Daulo Pass and Miunde which are a constant threat to human life and property and pose an obstacle to the smooth flow of trade and services.

Despite this inauspicious milieu, Simbu managed to be rated top in service delivery for those three consecutive years.

Skeptics claim it was mere paperwork and there was nothing on the ground to show for it. So I decided to chat with the Simbu head of education, Essy Walkaima, and seek his views.

Essy was cautious. "I don't want to engage in talks that have a political flavour," he said.

"If anyone is interested in knowing how my division delivers its services, he or she must come to my office. Otherwise its politics and it doesn't affect our service delivery credibility."

I persisted. But Simbu has beaten the resource rich provinces for three consecutive years. Is there a magic formula?

"There is no secret or magic formula for the success," Essy replied. "It is plain common sense. In this country, there is not one uniform service delivery model that is ideally suitable for all the provinces.

"Every province has to identify its own strengths and weaknesses and develop its own *modus operandi* that suits its own needs because the problems, obstacles and challenges faced by one province are not the same as those that are faced by others.

"Of course Waigani can develop national development policies and programs but when it comes to the nitty-gritty of implementing them, each province will have to decide for itself as to how best each can get the services through successfully under the prevailing circumstances on the ground."

Essy reminded me of casual conversations we'd had with Jimmy Drekore, Mathias Kin, Ware Mukale and others about the same matter.

We had concurred that Simbu would have to solve her own problems. The centre of government at Waigani could not solve Simbu's problems.

I believe the paramount reason for Simbu's success is her ability to innovate when the going gets tough.

The popular free tuition policy of the national government was the brainchild of Simbu. Simbu was the first province to introduce tuition free education in 1991 when the late David Mai Goro was premier.

The driving factor was hardship faced by parents in finding school fees. It was critical that something be done about it. The initiative relieved many parents of the school fee burden.

Simbus now working in PNG and abroad are the product of the fee-free concept.

The policy propelled David Mai to a landslide victory for the Simbu Regional seat in the 1992 national elections.

The poor internal revenue base meant that the policy placed an enormous strain on the health and transport sectors. Hence it was abolished a few years later.

Karimui has always been the greatest challenge in service delivery. Because of lack of road accessibility, remoteness and related hardships, public servants, especially teachers and health workers, used to abscond from duty. After a month or two, they sneaked away and never returned.

That's when innovation came into play. In 2007, the provincial education authorities and the former MP for Karimui Nomane, Posi Menai, entered into an agreement with Madang Teachers College to train Grade 10 school leavers from various parts of Karimui to become teachers.

Under the agreement, the school leavers were sent them to Madang Teachers College and, after graduation, they were sent back to Karimui to teach children in their own community.

The tuition fee for this project was paid by the Karimui Nomane District.

The only benefit this group of teachers gets is salary. There is no housing and leave airfares provided as they live in their own house in their own home village and teach.

"More than 30 Karimuians graduated through the scheme and are currently teaching in schools in Karimui," Essy told me.

"One of them was terminated for running away and teaching in the Eastern Highlands Province. This signaled a warning to others and they have all been very committed."

In health, all positions including community health workers, nurses and health extension officers in Karimui Nomane are two grades higher than health positions elsewhere. The additional benefit did the trick.

Looking at Simbu, it is not the Waigani service delivery models that produce desired results. Instead it is the creative approach taken by public servants in the province.

If Simbu can do that and achieve top results for three consecutive years then the methodology has something going for it.

6

Rationality and Calm Required on Bougainville Issue

APPARENTLY there is a lot of misunderstanding, confusion and misconception, especially among Bougainvilleans on the fundamental factors that became the impetus for the Paguna Copper Mine conflict. It is imperative that there must be more education on the fundamental factors that triggered the resentment and the subsequent crisis for better understanding, unity and progress.

Let me clarify my stance from the outset that I am not condoning the Bougainville crisis or its aftermath aspirations of Bougainvilleans. I am also mindful that wounds heal, memories fade but scars remain.

However, for a harmonious, balanced and none aggravating history on the crisis for those who know nothing about it and were born after the crisis (whether Bougainvilleans or other Papua New Guineans), the onus is on us to get the record right without the biased influence of egoistically indoctrinated ideologies.

This opening remark may be too harsh but I have got to be frank and realistic for written librettos have the power to make or break a nation. Remember the famous adage by Edward Bulwer-Lytton 'The pen is mightier than the sword'.

The Panguna deal is one that everybody that involved botched it up - the PNG Government including Bougainvillean members of the House of Assembly, the Australian government and the so-called advisers and Rio Tinto.

This was mainly attributed by the unfavourable fundamental factors on the ground which eventually became the nucleus of the whole crisis on the island.

First, the Panguna copper and gold mine was PNG's first big mining project that came about at the time when we were just beginning to transit from stone-age into modernization.

Our leaders including Bougainvillean members of the House of Assembly literally had no experience and skills in mining ventures. Our leaders were shoved a raw deal by the mining giant Rio Tinto and its subsidiary BCL.

Secondly, the public service machinery in general did not have the experience or the expertise to render sound advice to the government. We did not have qualified mining engineers and environmentalists and other experts as we have today to make an independent assessment of BCL's mining and environmental plans and advise the government effectively.

Thirdly, PNG needed money badly to develop a newly emerging country. As poor as we were at the time, Panguna was the golden opportunity that Konedobu could not allow it to slip by.

Fourthly, the land owners like our leaders and the rest of PNG at the time, had very little or no knowledge of the complexities. They were totally ignorant.

Fifthly, Rio Tinto, being one of the giants in the mining business at the time, with all its experience, clout and dominance, had the upper hand. Like I mentioned before, the people of PNG including the land owners were given a raw deal.

In the course of time as PNG progresses and interacts with the outside world and new knowledge and information became available to us, came to realize the mistakes of our leaders. That's when the resentment began to brew up.

Whether the BRA's call for hefty compensation and subsequently independence was rational and that all avenues of negotiations had been exhausted before sabotage and murder begun, I will not venture on to avoid digging the old graves. However, the pressure of arms built-up that had been going on for some years had to vent. It triumphed over sagacity – beginning with sabotage and the murder of innocent fellow Papua New Guineans from other provinces by Bougainvillean militants.

That led to the eventual all-out war that saw brothers fighting against brothers and sisters against sisters in Bougainville. No matter they were PNGDF soldiers, members of the BRA, members of the police force, correctional service officers or resistance fighters; they were all Papua New Guineans fighting each other.

All in all the preconditions on the ground back then were not in favour of equitable bargaining or resolution and the consequence was tragic. In light of this, it is futile vanity to point fingers at people of any one region or ethnic group.

The Panguna experience places the PNG government and land owners of all the other mines and fossil fuel projects in the country in a better position to strike equitable deals and will inform us in the future. This includes the reopening deal with BCL in Panguna.

Given these insights and the resultant resolution through the granting by PNG government of autonomous status for PNG's island of Bougainville, what raison d'etre is there for emasculating the peace accord and propagating a sensationalised separation ideology?

7

A Post Mortem of the Sukundumi Impasse

YESTERDAY I inadvertently came across the biography of the Grand Chief Sir Michael Somare in Wikipedia.

As I browsed, the memory unfolded of the political impasse between the Grand Chief and the O'Neill-Namah regime that almost brought Australia's closest neighbour and traditional friend, Papua New Guinea, into constitutional crisis and anarchy.

As reminiscences continued, I felt tranquillity sweep through my being. The most turbulent period in the political history of PNG apart from the Bougainville crisis had come to an end with peace and stability.

As we celebrate the New Year, we are on course.

The impasse and its related events are now all water under the bridge - the enactment of the controversial judicial conduct laws, the ousting of the Grand Chief from Parliament and his East Sepik provincial seat (subsequently regained at the general election), the military fracas and the storming of the National Court by Belden Namah in pursuit of the Chief Justice, Sir Salamo Injia.

Post-election, the Grand Chief buried the hatchet in Alotau and aligned himself and his national Alliance MPs with the coalition parties and made his former rival peter O'Neill the prime minister.

This humble act by the father of the nation prominently overshadowed all the outstanding constitutional references, court proceedings and other outstanding issues and paved the way for normalcy and stability.

As we know, PNG is the land of the unexpected and the most unfathomable and the weirdest scenes can unfold in any circumstance whether cultural, commercial, ethical or political.

Moreover, in PNG society, personal virtues and morals at leadership level and among the citizenry are not really important compared with western and other societies.

Like most people, I first thought Somare's u-turn decision was just one of those expect-the-unexpected PNG styles of response to circumstances and issues.

But as I continued to take knowledge of his entire biography, my conscience was troubled.

My mind was searching. How could the longest serving politician in the Commonwealth, the father of the nation, the warrior in his own right and the Sukundumi (the river god) of the Sepiks stoop that low and align himself with the rival under whose administration his personal reputation, clout and dominance were tarnished, humiliated, dragged and muddied?

How could he suddenly forgive him and join him as a friend?

Maybe he didn't have a third and better option.

However, in my pondering for a palatable rationale, another question popped up: Had the political marriage between Peter O'Neill's People's National Congress Party and Belden Namah's PNG Party continued into the July general elections and the formation of the new government, would the Grand Chief bury the hatchet and reconcile with them?

A statement made by former deputy prime minister and current opposition leader, Belden Namah, in his verbal war with current prime minister Peter O'Neill in their vying to form a new government struck my mind.

"I know how to make prime ministers. If I don't get the top post, I will make someone else become the prime minister".

Having delved into the credence of the statement, I am of the opinion that the Grand Chief knew something that the public did not know.

He knew who his real enemy was.

The political war was really the battle of the Sukundumis … Namah verses Somare, the river gods of the mighty Sepik River. It was a divide-and-fall saga of the Sepik dynasty.

The western Sukundumi, with his vast military experience, was the master tactician and frontline warrior fighting and dismantling the supremacy of the eastern Sukundumi with the support of a handful of erudite lieutenants – Sam Basil, Allan Marat, Powes Parkop and of course Peter O'Neill, to name a few.

Namah fought vigorously to defend what he fought for. This was evident in the words he spoke and the actions he took. The invasion of the sanctuary of the National Court in pursuit of the Chief Justice, and his personal quelling of the military fracas offer credible evidence.

Namah even went to the extreme of branding the Grand Chief a dinosaur when he declared his allegiance to Peter O'Neill in Alotau at the time of the formation of the new government.

All in all, the decision by Sir Michael and his MPs to bury the hatchet and to vote for Peter O'Neill for the prime minister against Belden Namah was nothing nobler than a learned and calculated payback … a continuation of the feud of the Sukundumis.

If the Grand Chief was genuine about burying the hatchet and moving on with life, he should have come face to face with his real foe, Belden Namah, and made a public reconciliation with him.

Only then the dark clouds hanging over his motives would

have cleared and there would be doubtless credence to his action. Christmas and New Year were the best times to do that.

8

Disrespectful Asylum Deal

This critique was written in remonstration against the Asylum Deal signed on the 9th of July 2013 between the then PM of Australia Kevin Rudd and his PNG counterpart Peter O'Neill in the lead up to the Australian Federal Election in September in which the Labour Party's Opposition Leader Tony Abbot won by landslide victory. Abbot became Australia's 25th Prime Minister and was sworn in on the 17th of September 2013. The Asylum Deal was partly responsible for Kevin Rudd's exit.

KEVIN Rudd's politically motivated agenda of dumping the asylum seeking boat people on PNG's soil should be reversed.

The deal between Rudd and PNG counterpart Peter O'Neill was done in a dubious manner and driven by the might of the Aussie dollar.

PNG PM Peter O'Neill was suborned by Rudd into blindly shouldering Rudd's politically motivated ludicrousness under the influence of the Aussie taxpayers' money without proper assessment of the long term implications on PNG.

Whether this is a temporal political ploy or otherwise, as far as the learned communities of the two countries are concerned, the deal is not properly and transparently done.

Even after so much public outcry, the deal still remains a secret. This is unbecoming of democracy and should be condemned in the strongest term for the deal to be reversed.

In the global community in which we live in, every nation depends on each another for commerce, trade, security and other bilateral and multilateral matters. There is no exception for PNG and Australia.

The PNG-Australia relationship is unique and it goes beyond the boundaries of any normal bilateral relationship of any two nations.

It has been more of a brotherly relationship that has had extended as far back as World War II when Papua New Guineans became wartime carriers for the Australian soldiers and even took up arms and fought alongside the Australians against the Japanese.

The relationship was further strengthened under the flagship of the colonial administration when thousands of young Australians toiled under horrendous conditions to bring civilization to the uncivilized and cannibalistic PNG... an effort that led to the subsequent granting of independence on 16 September 1975 without bloodshed.

Until now Australia has continued to enhance the relationship byway of aid. Until the 1980s, Australia pumped millions of dollars into the impoverished PNG coffers as direct budgetary support with no strings attached. PNG used the money as it pleased.

Later Canberra changed the aid policy to tied aid - projects under which PNG enjoys annual subvention of around half a billion dollars.

In view of these facts, I have always believed in my heart that Australia is PNG's best friend and will always remain our best friend. I am sure many Papua New Guineans and Australians would agree with me on this.

However, there are times that I get angry with Australia for certain Canberra-sponsored policies that are deemed detrimental yet are imposed on PNG.

One prime example was the Outcome-Based Education and now the asylum seeking boat people deal between our two prime ministers, Kevin Rudd and Peter O'Neill.

Australia has long been an asylum seekers' preferred country of destination. They have always headed for the shores of Australia; never PNG. Kevin Rudd and Peter O'Neill know that.

Now Rudd has shoved his politically-motivated egoistic agenda down the throat of O'Neill under the might of the Aussie dollar without regard for the views of the ordinary Papua New Guineans who will day to day bear the implications of the deal.

This to me is Australia as bully; emasculating the sovereignty of PNG and denying the intelligence of its people.

PNG politicians will always fall into the trap of 'free money' but Australia has a moral obligation to not set the pernicious bait at the first place.

This trend of Aussie dollar doing the talking without respect for the sovereignty of PNG as an independent nation will breed contempt and sour the relationship.

This pernicious approach by Australian politicians should be condemned in the strongest terms.

Mutual understanding and respect for each other's sovereignty and adherence to the wishes of the citizens of our respective countries must take precedence over money and other duress.

Then we will continue to enjoy a harmonious relationship between our two great nations.

9

Call Me Hot Head … The Science of Stepping On Toes

An Australian commenter labelled me as hot head from cloud 27th for my views on the asylum deal with Australia that I expressed (above) in PNG Attitude blog. I wrote this article in response to the personal attack.

I have just been honoured by persons who will go unmentioned, with the Hot Head Medal - a scintillating award for my views on the Kevin Rudd-sponsored asylum deal. Such are the perils of commentary.

I already had the hunch that I stepped on too many giant toes in the debate and I was expecting a direct fire much earlier but it came indirectly a bit late in a different scene. Nevertheless it came.

Whether my views on the issue are of any representation of the silent fellow Papua New Guineans or not, I am happy that I have the liberty to express my views freely and frankly, a privilege that most of my fellow Papua New Guinean Attitude readers are denied.

Being carefully observant, one would realize that my fellow Papua New Guinean Attitude readers are very selective in what they write and comment because they don't have the liberty like me to speak their mind freely.

Apart from a handful of fulltime students of the Devine Word University, most of them are professionals employed either by the state or private companies. They are subjected to the rules and code of ethics imposed on them by their employers.

They don't have the freedom to speak their hearts' feelings on highly sensitive political issues concerning PNG and Australia because of repercussions if they are not careful in what they say. This is a limitation of free speech for them.

For an unemployed, mischievous hot head like me, I have nothing to lose for speaking out rightly and such naming emboldens me. Only if I had committed a cardinal crime then I would have cowered into the hellish shit hole.

However, the despicable crime that I detest to commit especially in public media is to harm anyone by making personal allusions and backlash. Keith Jackson has reminded us on several occasions that we all have a moral obligation to observe that this is not happening.

Anyone can become red hot head on issues and that's that and is end of the story. Leonard Fong Roka and self-locked horns of ideological differences on certain Bougainville issues and that's that. There were no personal allusions and backlash between us. That's the beauty of debates and commentaries on issues in public media.

Hot heads, tepid heads, cool heads and whatever heads us all produce in the literature, commentary and debate on PNG Attitude are lively, colourful, meaningful, beneficial and enjoyable. How would it be if we all had cool heads or spongy - malomalo heads?

10

If Dekla Says PNG is Eden, Then It Is

This article was in an indirect response to an Australian journalist calling PNG a shithole in one of the Australian media. The article won the 2013 PNG Chamber of Mines and Petroleum Crocodile Prize Essay Award.

IN need of vitamin D from heaven's abundant supply, I wheeled in my battered wheelchair down to the helipad at the far southern end of the Sir Joseph Nombri Memorial hospital Kundiawa which is my home. As I was sun bathing, Kaupa, an old friend and an aspiring politician, walked up to me. He had seen me through the window of the ward where his sick daughter was admitted the day before. We chattered for a while and Kaupa suggested that we go to the hospital front-gate market for a cup of Kongo coffee. He helped me push my wheelchair and we went to the favourite coffee spot.

After a cup each at Dorothy's coffee shop, I was tempted to take a chew of the betel nut. We moved to the first seller on the Wara Simbu side of the road and I paid for two nuts.

As we were chewing, a young woman in her early thirties came towards us wearing, a six-pocket trouser, collared tee-shirt and a pair of strappers.

"Dekla, my sister, what are you doing here?" the buai seller asked the woman in Tok Pisin.

"My sister Paula, it's been a long time." Dekla responded and they shook hands.

"I've been in the hospital for some days now looking after my son. He twisted his ankle while playing with other children and he got admitted", Dekla explained.

After chatting with Paula for a while, Dekla asked her for some betel nut. "Sista sampela piksa buai o - sister any display nuts?"

"Sista laip em had tru - sister life is so difficult. Buai em ino planti - betel nuts are not plenty. Yu baim na kaikai - you buy and chew", the buai seller responded.

"Sista, mi askim long wanpela piksa buai tasol - sister, I am asking for a display nut only. Blong wanem yu tok laip i had - why are you saying life is so difficult? Olsem wanem laip i had tru ... how comes life is so difficult?"

"Sori sista, laip long taun i had tru ... sorry sister, life in town is so hard. Olgeta samting i moni tasol - everything is money".

"Oh sista, yu nogat wok na yu hangamap nating long town olsem na yu painim laip em had ... oh sister, yu have no jobs and you are just squatting in town that's why you find life so difficult. Yu mas kam bek long ples ... you must come back to the village.

"Ples em heven ...village is heaven. Olgeta samting i stap ... everything is in the village. Yu ino bai wari long wanpela samthing ... you will never be worried about anything".

The conversation turned into an argument and became quite bitter so I decided to distract them. I gave K2 to Paula and instructed her to give Dekla four nuts worth 50 toea each.

Dekla looked at me and shook her head. "Give his money back" she said and pulled the K2 off from Paula's hand and gave it back to me.

"I feel sorry for you. I have money. I will buy myself some nuts but not from this rubbish" and Dekla pulled out a K10 note out of a stake of ten and twenty kina bills in her purse in full view of Paula and walked to the next seller. Would you like a drink, coke? She asked me and I nodded.

From the corner of my eyes I saw Paula swallowed a lump that refused to go down her throat. I couldn't figure out what was going on in her mind but clearly she was flustered.

Dekla came back with a bottle of coke and a hand full of betel nut and mustard beans to where we were. She gave me the coke and suggested that we stay under the shade of the mango tree on the other side of the road and chew. We agreed and went to the shade of the mango tree.

"Paula is my cousin", Dekla explained as she and Kaupa were chewing the nuts and I was drinking the coke.

"We are from Toromambuno in Gembogl. We both left school after completing grade six and got married.

"Me and my husband we live in the village. Our three children were born at Gembogl rural health centre.

"Once in a while I travel to Madang or Lae to sell my carrots, broccoli and cauliflowers. After selling them, I buy clothes and household items - mattresses, blankets and cooking pots - that we need and I go back.

"Paula and her husband left the village soon after they got married and they have been living in a settlement around here ever since.

"I don't understand this talk of hard life or poverty. May be this is the language of vagrants squatting in settlements in towns and cities.

"In the village, we have everything we need. We have food, fresh clean water, firewood and, house to live in.

"When we are hungry, we just take a walk to the back of our house and pick ripe bananas, avocado or sugar cane and consume them and we are full.

"When we need salt, soap, kerosene, cooking oil or a Flex Card to make a phone call, we pick coffee or vegetables from the garden and sell them on the roadside, get the money and we buy these things.

"We are not worried about money. We don't struggle in the scorching heat to make a few kinas for just one evening's meal.

"We do gardening whenever we feel like. Otherwise we go washing in the creek or lazing around with friends and play 7 Bomb - cards. We are happy.

"I feel sorry for my sister and her family. They must come back to the village" Dekla said.

I was very interested in what Dekla said especially after all the negative publicity about PNG in the Australian media. I mulled over what she said for a while and then asked her; "Dekla, contrary to what you have said, some Australians are saying that PNG is a poverty stricken shithole. What do you think about that?" I stressed every word for effect.

"What?" Kaupa and Dekla fumed simultaneously.

"Lucky their (Australians) jobless are living off the dole otherwise they would have starved to death". So said Kaupa, the senior public servant and aspiring politician.

"People like Paula who live in settlements and lack basic needs like food, good shelter and descent clothes may come under the definition of poverty Australians are talking about. But that's only a fraction of the whole population. Most Papua New Guineans, including me and my people in Salt Nomane, are not poor.

"We don't survive on dole handout. We don't live in makeshift tents. We don't survive on a spoonful of donated rice and soup day by day. We don't stand in queue for hours just to get a bucket of water for a week".

Dekla cut in. "You are right my brother. Papua New Guinea is Eden. We don't lack anything, so why outsiders should describe us as poor people".

I intervened and changed the subject. After all, the nuts were depleted. We dispersed. And I forgot about the incident.

Some days later, Phil Fitzpatrick's article *PNG: The Australian Media's Mad … I love the place* appeared in PNG Attitude and reminded me of the conversation. I thought readers might like to make their own judgment.

11

Removing Tambaran Carvings a Stepping Stone to Change

THE opponents of the removal of carvings and art work at the National Parliament under the direction of the Speaker Hon. Theo Zurenuoc have ignored two important facts in their arguments.

First, the National Parliament is not a museum. The right place for preservation of historical relics, carvings and all kinds of cultural heritage is in a museum and not the National Parliament.

All the carvings that are being taken down at the Parliament can always find their rightful place at the National Museum and Art Gallery which is nearby. No problem.

Parliament House is a modern structure based on modern political ideology and as such the structure and the face of it can be altered at any time to suit development and change.

In fact the idea of removing all those ugly, scary and evil looking idols is not new. It has been mooted by parliamentarians, civil society and Christians for some years and it is so happens that the practicality of it has eventuated during the tenure as speaker of Theo Zurenuoc. At least he had the guts to sanction the project.

Secondly, I wonder if anyone has seriously thought about the meaning of tambaran and its attachment to the National Parliament. Tambaran is the Tok Pisin word for evil spirit or demon and all the bad connotations that associated with it.

Why is the National Parliament called Haus Tambaran –

Haus of Demon? The answer lies with all those fierce carvings perceived to guard the entrance to the Parliament House and the Parliament itself. It is those living spirits with fixed abodes as they are called by Grand Chief Sir Michael Somare that gives us the depiction, Haus Tambaran.

The National Parliament is a noble and honorable institution that operates on Christian principles, or supposed to be, and it should never have been called Haus Tambaran. It is proper for the name Haus Tambaran and all its associations to be uprooted and erased from the face of the Parliament and in the minds of the people. The Speaker has done the right thing.

Papua New Guinea as an independent nation has declared its allegiance to the Jehovah God, the God of Israel, and the significance of it are manifested in the preamble of the Constitution and the Constitution itself which is based on Christian principles.

The National Parliament, the country's most important institution, should depict Christianity from the entrance into the interior. The entrance should have murals of archangels with swords in their hands guarding it and not all those fierce and scary idols. They should be guarding the entrance of the National Museum and Art Gallery and not the Parliament house.

Furthermore, the greatest teacher of all time, Jesus Christ, said about the power of spoken words: You speak words and they will come to pass. We call the National Parliament a house of evil and truly it is full of evil – extreme corruption. The evil will continue to reign if we do not do something about it. What the speaker is doing is right.

Of course we all want our leaders to change their attitude and mindset to God fearing and accountable in managing the affairs of the country. However changing the attitude and mindset of our leaders directly is not so easy and even a small project such as this can be a stepping stone towards evoking changes and making difference.

12

An Overdue and Judicious Remuneration Policy for Magistrates

THE O'Neill-Dion government has allocated K38.4 million in the 2014 national budget for the remuneration of the 4800 officials of the 1600 village courts throughout Papua New Guinea. This is a judicious policy of recompense that needs to be sustained by successive national governments in future.

In a country where the bulk of her population dwells in small, scattered and isolated communities across rugged terrains where civilization is still a dream and the presence of government is literally zero, village courts are often the only evidence of tangible governance; maintaining order and peace in what could have been an anarchic state of affairs.

Established under the Village Courts Act of 1973, the village courts came into operation in 1975, the year that Papua New Guinea gained independence. It is the foundation of the country's four-tier judicial system: Village, District, National and Supreme Courts.

The personnel comprised a magistrate who mediates over disputes, a court clerk who is a record keeper and a peace officer who assists the court and enforces its decisions.

The core function is to ensure peace and harmony in the area for which it is established by mediating in, and endeavouring to obtain just and amicable settlement of disputes.

Specific offences within the court's jurisdiction include striking, using insulting words, property damage, drunkenness, failure to perform customary duties or obligations and sorcery.

A village court may order compensation of up to K300 but without any limit in cases regarding custody of children, bride price or compensation for deaths.

Despite difficulties like formality of procedures, complicated application of customs, unofficial dispute resolution, lack of supervision by District Court magistrates, these are important courts that have effectively served one third of PNG for the last 38 years.

A positive sentiment was expressed in The Report on Law and Order in Papua New Guinea and I quote: "While there are no objective measures, it seems likely that village courts are contributing to the maintenance of order by assisting in the peaceful settlement of disputes and proving quicker and surer punishment for minor offenders ...

"[T]hey have provided a spur to the sense of community and involvement in community, and to a sense of the worth of the things run by and for common people. Insofar as they are successfully linked to other government agencies, village courts contribute to the legitimacy of the state and hence to the other sources of order in the country at large."

For the love of job and welfare of their people, village court officials perform their functions devotedly even under difficult and risky conditions. At times they become victims of the work they do.

For instance in 2012, a village court magistrate from Kup in the Simbu Province was reported to have been gunned down in an ambush - mistaken for enemy when he was on his way to broker peace between two warring tribes.

In November 2013, a motor vehicle belonging to the chairman of the Goroka Urban Joint Village Court was reported to have had been torched in relation to a case he chaired some days earlier.

There have been many such reports and they reflect the perils of the work of the courts. And guess how much magistrates have been getting for the drudgery? A lousy K24- 32 a month. They were paid in lump sum once or twice a year.

Many of them had to spend substantial amounts of money on transport to collect the paltry allowance. For example, village court officials from Nomane LLG in the Simbu province spent K100 on PMV to travel to Kundiawa, collect their allowance and return. This is equivalent to five months' allowance. Meals and accommodation were extras.

Consider areas like Karimui, Marawaka, Telefomin and others that are accessible only by air; the average return air fare is around K300 and it is not worth the expense or the risk. It was farcically uneconomical to pursue collecting the fee.

In most instances, the village court officials performed their jobs without worrying about their allowance. The council presidents and the district officials have access to the provincial headquarters and they got the pay and kept it for themselves.

The only benefit magistrates' depend on and will continue to do so is the K50 court fines paid by the plaintiffs and defendants.

Despite the poor pay, magistrates have been relentlessly loyal to their work. While some of the pioneer magistrates and peace officers have passed on or retired, others have survived the test of time. They have been through thick and thin and to this very day are still maintaining law and order in their communities.

One of these stalwarts is Tabai Philip of Yobai Village Court in Salt Nomane. He became a magistrate when the Village Court was first introduced to the area in 1977 and has been the chairman of the joint sitting ever since.

I met Tabai in Kundiawa Town on the eve of the New Year and asked him how he felt about the new remuneration and he promptly replied: "This is the first time that the national government has recognised the importance of the Village Courts and the value of the service we workers have been rendering to the community and the nation in a momentous way. I am very happy".

Tabai's sentiment is a reflection of the general feelings among the village court workers throughout the country.

I asked him about how much they would be paid and a jubilant Tabai replied: "Mipela i no save yet tasol tokwin i olsem mipela bai kisim samting olsem K200 i go long K300 long wan-wan fotnait [We don't know yet but the rumour is that we will be paid something like K200 - K300 a fortnight]".

We are now in 2014 and the Prime Minister Peter O'Neill proclaimed this week that this is the year of implementation of his governments' policies. Can the new remuneration for the village courts come into effect in January to give credence to the prime minister's statement and policy?

More importantly, can this worthy policy be sustained in the years to come? The history of PNG politics has shown that the demise of the reigning government is the demise of its major policies.

However, such a fate should not meet this policy for it is judicious that, regardless of who is in power, it must be valued and sustained as long as the Village Court exists.

13

The Street People for Whom There Is No Tomorrow

THE problem of orphans is getting serious that the government cannot ignore it any more. The number of waifs and strays on the streets is constantly on the rise.

As you travel around the cities and towns of PNG today, you will notice the faces of young children mainly between the ages of 6 and 12 going from street to street collecting empty cans and bottles and, doing small errands for a few toea to buy flour balls for the evening.

If they are lucky, a cup of coffee complements the flour balls. Otherwise cold water suffices.

Amongst the young people, you will see some elderly males and females also collecting empty cans and bottles all in determination for survival. Many of them grew up as waifs and strays in the slums.

For these people there is no tomorrow. All they care about is today.

Talk to them about the 2015 Pacific Games or the multibillion kina LNG project coming on line in 2014. To them they are meaningless stories. All they see is bleak despondency. What they care about is their immediate need for the day.

They have no place to call home. The way they dress and the filth and the stench of unwashed bodies would clearly tell that they do not belong to a proper home.

They lodge with wantoks in overcrowded squalid cardboard shelters or they hang around night clubs or gambling dens in the slums until dawn. In the morning they are back on the street and the routine continues.

When the going gets tough, what is good and what is bad become obliterated. Pocket picking, shoplifting, bag snatching and mob attacks become necessary. Crime and violence are on the rise.

Girls are turning to prostitution in their teens.

HIV and AIDS is the biggest contributor to the orphan problem. As parents die of AIDS and other calamities, the number of orphans increases.

The Chairman of the National AIDS Council Dr Banare Bun revealed in Kokopo last week that the total number of population infected with HIV stands at 35, 000. This is official figure excludes those who have not been tested and recorded.

Most of them are young people within the ages of 15 to 25 years and most are married.

When parents die of AIDS, they leave their very young children to grandparents and wantoks who generally do not take good care of them. The children are abused and mistreated.

As a result, they are forced to the streets to fend for themselves.

Prime Minister Peter O'Neill is 'compassionate' about the welfare of so-called asylum seekers - foreigners of unknown background most of who are wilfully leaving their country for greener pastures in Australia.

Peter O'Neill is ignoring his own people in dire need of government attention.

The problem is getting worse by the year and the government cannot continue to ignore it. The welfare of Papua New Guineans should take precedence over that of foreigners with the aid money from Australia and elsewhere.

If ordinary people can see the problem and go out of their way to address it, then the problem is serious. The Mother of Life Centre in Simbu Province founded by Martin Van der Palen of Netherland, the Faith Based Orphanage (Outreach) in Western Highlands Province run by Aunty Ruth and the Nangbe Nazarene Care Centre in the Jiwaka Province operated by husband and wife Steven and Ruth are good examples.

There are also several other care centres established and operated by ordinary people to care for orphans and their needs.

The three centres mentioned each look after an average of 50 to100 children a year. This figure may be insignificant compared with the total problem, but the important thing is they have seen the problem and gone out of their way to address it.

The availability of resources - land space, shelter, food and of course money - is the biggest challenge.

Out of compassion and benevolence, they voluntarily have taken the burden upon themselves to provide shelter, food, clothing and education for the children.

These organisations are providing a noble service which is rightfully the responsibility of government. It is a mammoth task that these charities are tackling and the government cannot continue to turn a blind eye.

The government must provide support through the District Services Improvement Program with yearly grant assistance for sustenance and expansion until such time as the government has an orphanage policy in place

The sooner the better this is.

14

Forget Dutch Disease; Fossil Fuel Boom Much Needed

This article was written in response to the general fear of a trigger of Dutch Disease in Papua New Guinea as a result of the country's fossil fuel boom particularly Exxon Mobil's multibillion LNG project in the Southern Highlands that started in 2010 [and came into production in April 2014].

DUTCH Disease has become a concern in recent times amongst economists, policymakers, politicians, bloggers and others particularly for economies like Papua New Guinea that are currently experiencing a boom in fossil.

The phrase Dutch disease was coined by The Economist magazine in 1977 to describe the Netherlands' economic crisis of the 1960s and 1970s.

A large deposit of oil was discovered in the North Sea. The sudden new found wealth (high foreign currency earnings) forced the Dutch's guilder to appreciate making other Dutch's exports expensive and none competitive on the world market.

One sector's meat turned out to be other sectors' poison.

In Canada, the debate on Dutch disease has been raging on for quite some time and is centred on the oil riches of Alberta, Newfoundland and Labrador and the decline in Canada's manufacturing industry.

"Canada does have Dutch disease" says Organisation for Economic Cooperation and Development, the world's largest economic watchdog.

"Forget Dutch disease, we're In the Money", says Mark Carney, Governor of the Bank of Canada, in a counter argument.

"Don't blame Alberta for Ontario's manufacturing woes", says yet another group, and the debate goes on.

The proponents of Dutch disease are saying that the appreciation in the Canadian dollar as a result of the oil boom is responsible for the decline in manufacturing industry.

The opponents say that the decline in the manufacturing industry has been a global phenomenon for both no-oil and oil rich countries for decades and has nothing to do with the oil boom.

The United State is not unaffected. An article by Brad Plummer of Washington Post ('U.S. Oil production is booming. Is Dutch Disease on the way?' 19 March 2013) states; "The US is suddenly awash in fossil fuels. Oil output has risen to its highest level since 1992. Natural gas is booming, thanks to new and improved tracking techniques, which means it's time to worry about Dutch disease".

In Israel, Steven Scheer writes in a Reuters report (14 April 2013); "Israel's cabinet on Sunday April 14, re-approved the establishment of a sovereign wealth fund (SWF) to prevent Dutch disease once natural gas fields (referring to the Tamar natural gas which reported to have reserves of some 10 trillion cubic feet that began production in March and the nearby larger Leviathan field that sets to come on line early 2016) start to generate high level of income".

In Papua New Guinea, Exxon Mobil's $19 billion liquefied natural gas project is reported to be set for production in 2014. The maximum annual output of 6.9 million tons forecast for 2015 and beyond is on target which means Papua New Guinea is heading into the high end of its fossil fuel foreign exchange earnings.

Sentiments about Dutch disease in PNG have been mooted since 2008. Among the list of concerned institutions have been the World Bank, the Bank of PNG, Manufacturer's Council of PNG and the Development Blog.

There is a general agreement among analysts and commentators that Dutch disease is here in PNG. Some have based their views on the empirical tenet that Dutch disease has its root in fossil fuel boom. Others have cited the decline in the agriculture sector as the basis.

PNG's agriculture sector is highly trade sensitive and has always been vulnerable to local currency and world commodity price movements. Although the latter have backed it up with statistical evidence. Papua New Guinea is an insignificant player on the world agriculture commodity market. It has no influence over the prices of its agricultural exports like coffee, cocoa, copra, palm oil and timber.

This means that the appreciation of the kina, either as a result of fossil fuel boom or currency fixation by government regulation, puts PNG's agriculture sector under threat. Thus to jump the gun and employ the gloomy theory of Dutch disease in PNG is a long shot.

Forget Dutch disease and focus on the enormous benefits the country's fossil fuel wealth will bring to this impecunious nation when Exxon's PNG natural gas project comes on line in 2014. Imports will be cheaper. There will be increased spending on infrastructure development and social services meaning improved living standards and greater economic security for the country.

Our chief concerns should be about prudent fiscal and financial policies and management of the windfall that will cushion the kina appreciation, mitigating the decline in the agriculture and other sectors and bringing about maximised infrastructure development and social service benefits - preventing the so-called Dutch disease.

The sovereign wealth fund which the PNG Government has already sanctioned will hold part of the windfall in savings or investments to not only cushion the currency appreciation but to create long term economic security for PNG. We have taken the right direction in that.

A second strategy is to use part of the windfall to invest in the agriculture sector by way of subsidies and bounties. [Agriculture has been the keystone of survival in PNG and putting revenue from the extractable industry into this sector would do a million good things for the bulk of our population whose welfare depends on agriculture].

Third is the equitable benefit sharing of the windfall. One way is a 100% tuition fee subsidy for all levels of education. School fees are the number one burden for 85% of the rural population. A total tuition fee subsidy will do a hundred good things for them and Dutch disease will mean nothing to them.

15

Oil Search Share Acquisition a Strategic Investment for PNG

THE Papua New Guinea government's 10.01 % share acquisition in Oil Search with A$1.2 billion UBS (United Bank of Sweden) loan is a vital investment for the people of PNG. For ages we have been complaining about multinational companies reaping our natural resources and giving us scraps ... so rich yet so poor has been our cry for donkey's years. The gas and oil business is booming. Apart from Exxon Mobil's LNG Project, in which the PNG government holds a 17% stake, InterOil's Elk and Antelope gas fields - described as the country's largest gas deposits - are about to be developed. And there could be more gas and oil elsewhere. So how can we get equity for our citizens and maximise our gains?

The best option is increased participation by the people either directly or indirectly through the elected government and prime minister Peter O'Neill has just done that.

I cannot think of another better or more innovative way for participation by the people, particularly the poor rural masses.

The majority of our people are poor and do not have the capital to directly invest in the gas and oil business. As a result, they have been mere bystanders, gaining very little benefit in the form of royalties although admittedly there has been employment, contracts and taxes.

Through this latest investment, Papua New Guineans, who in their lifetime would have never acquired direct shareholding in the lucrative oil and gas sector, now own a 10.01% stake in Oil Search through their elected government.

This means that, apart from royalties and taxes, PNG will also benefit from Oil Search's profits, in the form of dividends, for the next 50 plus years.

Debt financing is a normal investment practice, however the concern people express is whether the government has mortgaged its future earnings from its 17% stake in the PNG Project.

It is highly likely that Peter O'Neill did mortgage the future earnings because in any such large commercial loan there has to be collateral and in this case UBS would require it.

Nonetheless, profitability and the ability to repay are determining factors in this kind of investment. People who question this matter are indirectly questioning the integrity of Exxon and Oil Search, the two companies the state has an interest in.

With the expected revenue of K75 bullion over the next 30 years, the loan debt of K8 billion is manageable.

The fear of the loan having a negative impact on the broader economy is unnecessary as it will be amortised over a number of years thus spreading the debt burden and easing any strain on the economy.

It is nonsense to suggest such a large loan will be amortised in just two or three years.

Making comparisons with unprofitable state owned enterprises to give credence to one's negative argument on the investment is a flawed tactic.

All the SOEs are controlled and influenced by the government while this investment is totally different in nature and beyond state influence, hence the prospect of success looks good. Otherwise, again, we might be questioning the integrity and strength of Exxon and Oil Search.

Moreover, partnering with the largest oil and gas company in the country and a publicly listed (POMX and ASX) firm, the purchase is a worthwhile and strategically selective investment.

Oil Search is a PNG-registered entity founded in 1929 and operating five oil fields (Kutubu, Moran, Gobe, Mananda and Iagifu-Hedina) and one gas field (Hides), all in the highlands.

The company has a 29% interest in the soon-on-line $US 15.7 billion PNG LNG Project and, with the recent acquisition of 22.8% stake in PNG's largest undeveloped gas fields, Elk and Antelope gas fields in the Gulf Province, the company is set to quadruple its profit in 2014 and onwards.

The people of PNG through their elected government are strategically positioned to benefit immensely from its growth.

I would be against the government if it decided to invest likewise in sectors of the economy other than gas and oil. This is a strategically sound and good investment.

My concern is the manner in which the prime minister sacked William Duma and Don Polye as Petroleum Minister and Treasurer respectively and appointed himself acting Treasurer to pave the way for expediting the loan agreement and purchasing shares.

However, I think the timing factor had a lot to do with these decisions.

16

Disastrous Upshots: Wantokism and Business in PNG

THERE are many factors that contribute to the downfall or lack of development of small to medium businesses by Papua New Guineans however, I will touch on the two core ones and they are lack of management and wantokism.

Poor management of money and time are the big time killers of SMEs in this country. In most SMEs, there is no demarcation and independence between the owners and the business. They are one.

When the owner or his family need money, they get it from the business without paying it back and thus making the business cash flow suffer until it fails completely.

To avoid this from happening, the owner must treat business as an independent entity and pay himself or herself wages.

Furthermore, most small enterprise owners don't treat their business as fulltime job. They operate on ad hoc basis. As the popular saying goes, time is money. The more time is dedicated to a business, the more money it is going to make and thus the opportunity for growth.

Wantokism or the wantok system is a phenomenon that impacts every sphere of life in Papua New Guinean society, including business.

In traditional PNG society, wantokism operated as a welfare buffer and underpinned social security. It ensured no one went hungry or was naked or homeless.

Everyone made sure that all other people, including those who were vulnerable and disadvantaged, had food to eat, clothes to wear and a shelter or a place to live.

Wantokism tied and held together the tenet and communal principles of a clan or tribe. It instilled clanship and the tribal bond. It was a good custom.

But the application of wantokism in the modern socio-economic sphere tends to entail more disastrous upshots than good.

When it comes to meeting traditional obligations like compensation and bride price payments and funeral expenses, the community expects the wantok businessmen and women to make significant contributions.

They are expected to contribute competitively and above other contributions to live up to and maintain respect and status in the community. Fear of being cursed and sorcery is also involved in this decision.

Business owners are often compelled to misappropriate money that is vital asset to the growth and expansion of the enterprise. As a result, small businesses go into bankruptcy or fail to expand.

Those entrepreneurs who operate outside of and away from traditional community ties and customary influences are most likely to prosper.

There are many businesses that could have reached one million kina turnover, but were destroyed in tribal fights and ethnic clashes because of wantokism.

Workshops, trade stores, liquor clubs, coffee plantations, factories and PMV buses owned by innocent people were destroyed because the owners were wantoks of one idiot drunkard or marijuana addict who murdered or harmed someone from a different clan, tribe or ethnic group.

In 1996, all the Eastern Highlanders living in Mt Hagen were chased out and their businesses worth hundreds of thousands of kina were torched to ashes by locals because one Western Highlander was murdered by an Eastern highlander.

Lae City is the hub of ethnic clashes. The main characters are Morobeans and Western Highlanders. They have clashed several times in the past and businesses, particularly buses and tucker shops owned by Western Highlanders were torched.

Moreover, if you haven't heard this before, there is such a thing as a wantok price in PNG. If your wantok is a sales person or sales manager in a business, you are likely to get what you want at a very high discount or even free.

In a fast food shop you can get a free a plate of chicken and chips and a cola worth K20 if your wantok is in charge. This is real and I have seen it with my own eyes.

This is the wantok price and this is how bad the wantok system operates in PNG today. No wonder the Asians are successful because they keep their eyes on the till from 6 am to 6 pm 7 days a week.

Then there is wantokism in job recruitment and placement. Unqualified wantoks are given jobs resulting in poor performance and low productivity, a phenomenon that we know is very common in government departments in this land of the unexpected.

The PNG government realises the high rate of poverty and general failure or lack of development of SMEs by our people.

In its bid to address the problems and promote a business culture in PNG, the government has injected millions of kina into state economic development agencies, namely the Small Business

Development Corporation, Department of Agriculture, National Fisheries Authority and National Development Bank to facilitate training, technical assistance, grants and low interest micro-credit facilities.

The Small Business Development Corporation, in liaison with provincial commerce officials, is vigorously carrying out a training program called Start Your Own Business (SYOB), for small provincial entrepreneurs, NGOs, women's groups and so on.

One course was conducted in Kundiawa early this year exclusively for women. A total of 120 Simbu women from all walks of life (subsistence farmers, public servants, small business entrepreneurs) attended the two weeks course and graduated with a certificate.

The Minister for Trade and Commerce Richard Maru was guest of honour at the graduation ceremony.

The government also realises that cooperative business societies have improved a lot in their operations lately.

Thus the state is promoting cooperative business societies through technical support, training and finance.

At least the government of the day has realised the problems and in its wisdom has adopted the appropriate measures.

It is up to Papua New Guinean businessmen and women to distinguish the difference between business ethics and wantokism and set clear demarcations between them in their day to day operations. Only then can they prosper and run shoulder to shoulder with the foreigners in their entrepreneurship.

17

How to Break Free from the Vicious Cycle of Dinau

LIVING on borrowed money is a big problem for thousands of workers in Papua New Guinea today.

Approximately three quarters of the working population in this country are so enslaved by dinau that they find it extremely difficult to break free from its grip. Dinau kilim mi ya (debts are killing me) is a national sentiment among the work force.

People who earn less than a thousand kina a fortnight and are single breadwinners with large families are the most affected. Gamblers, alcohol users and cigarette and betel nut consumers are doomed without borrowed money.

The vicious cycle of dinau evolves from the squandering of take-home fortnightly income (after tax, bank loans etc. have been deducted) on unbudgeted non-essentials like alcohol, cigarettes, betel nut, customary and extended family obligations and gambling on the pokies, horse races, cards and the lottery.

Papua New Guineans know how to budget their income mentally or in written form. However, the problem is, they have the high tendency of not adhering to their budgets. They spend indiscriminately. As a result they run out of money for necessities like food, fuel and bus fare well before the next pay packet arrives.

To provide for these basic needs they have to find money somehow. The easiest and fastest way is to borrow from the fast-growing money laundering business known as moni maket at exorbitant fortnightly interest rates of 30, 40 or even 50 or 100 percent.

The usurers readily lend as long as the loan seekers agree to the interest charged and at the same time surrender their EFTPOS cards along with pin codes enabling the money lenders to collect their dues directly from the ATMs.

The prevailing trend is that when the previous loan is repaid, new financial pressures bite into the family budget forcing the breadwinner to borrow again. Each time, consciously or unconsciously, the loan increases until the total debt comprising the principal plus interest reaches an unmanageable proportion. Often the debt equals or exceeds the take-home income of the breadwinner-cum-debtor.

The vicious circle of debt comes into effect at this point. The money lender has the upper hand, taking the entire take-home income of the borrower. The poor person then borrows again from the money usurers to sustain his or her family's life and they go round and round like that payday after payday.

The consequence on the social and economic welfare of workers and their families are diverse. Non-payment of children's school fees, disconnection of electricity and water supplies, sale of household items like TV sets and prostitution by female family members are some common consequences. The extremes are court proceedings and loss of jobs when the borrowers try to evade their loans by getting new EFPTOS cards with new pin codes, electronic transfer through phone banking or, running away to new locations and new jobs.

How can people who have been enslaved by debts for many years break free of its grip? Before embracing any plan, it is of paramount importance that one must have the willpower to break free. Having your heart and mind fully committed to breaking free is the catalyst for any plan to be fruitful because most plans will involve self-discipline and sacrifices.

Once your heart and mind are fixed then you should list down all the possible means and ways and assess them one by one. Eventually you should come up with one best option to follow.

My recommendation would be lifestyle adjustment – making adjustments or changes to one's style of living. There are two components to the lifestyle adjustment plan.

First is cost saving through budget cuts. You must cut down on spending on the non-essentials mentioned above as well as other expenses. What the percentage to be slashed on each item is up to the individual to decide.

I would recommend 50 % cuts on alcohol, cigarettes, betel nut and customary and extended family obligations. I strongly recommend a 100% cut on gambling, meaning a complete stop. Reduce communication by 40%. Reduce electricity and water rates and fuel like kerosene and petrol or diesel for private motor vehicles by at least 25%.If you are renting accommodation it is worth searching around for a cheaper home. The list is not exhaustive. You can add more.

The second component that complements the cost saving measures is a change of habits.

You must avoid those people you used to drink, chew and gamble with as much as possible. Avoid entering into long conversations with them. Say hi, see you later and move on. If you don't do that the temptation of the old habits and peer pressure will drag you back to square one. You will get nowhere.

Do not go near your favourite drinking and gambling dens especially on pay days and weekends. Take your family to the park, beach, rivers, sporting event or church fellowship.

You must boldly set boundaries to customary and extended family obligations and pressures and stand by your decision. You must have the guts to say no to their unreasonable demands.

You must stop calling or receiving calls from phone friends who have been flirtatiously enticing you into sending credits and cash. Twenty kina can save your family one decent meal.

You must talk openly about your problems and your intentions with your relatives and friends, including your old drinking, chewing and gambling mates. They must understand why you have changed your spending and social habits. Their understanding, respect and cooperation are important for the success of your plan.

Speed up your loan repayments by making additional repayments with 50% of the money you have saved fortnightly from your cost saving measures.

If you strictly adhere to your break-free plan, you will find that your financial position and social habits have significantly improved. Your debts will have gone in six to twelve months. You will have surplus money in your account to meet your family needs before the next pay packet arrives. You can easily manage your children's school fee loans without jeopardizing your family's welfare.

Once you have broken free from the grip of the vicious circle of debt, it is important that you maintain it.

Be very careful of the old habits because, to many people, they [old habits] are as sweet as honey. They can't live without them.

If you get back into the vicious cycle, you might never get out of it again for the rest of your life.

Look for books and articles on money management and budget tips in the libraries, internet, bookshops, newspapers and magazines and read them. They will help you to properly manage your finance because the debt problem stems from your poor management of your hard earned cash.

A good piece of general advice to the current and future workforce is that you must budget your take-home fortnightly income scrupulously and strictly adhere to it until the next pay packet arrives. Live within your means and you will never get into debt.

18

The Corrosive Effect of Westernisation on Nuptial Traditions

AMONG the problem that exist in marriage in Papua New Guinea today are the domino effects of disintegration and adulteration of customary nuptial principles by the callous forces of westernisation.

The other day I was returning from town back to Sir Joseph Nombri Memorial Hospital where I live.

Beside the road at Agua Market, I noticed a commotion. People were shouting obnoxious language. My helper (wheelchair pusher) and I stopped to find out what was going on.

A mother and her son in-law were having a fracas and the mother was berating and directing all kinds of invective at her in-law.

"Lukim em, sem blong em – Look at him, shame on him. Wanem taim bai yu baim Susan – When are you going to pay for Susan? Karim pikinini nating na nogat pay; yu mas sem long yu yet – Producing children without paying the bride price; you must be ashamed of yourself.

"Nogat wok, nogat haus, pipia karim pikinini nating olsem dog – No job, no home, rubbish bearing children senselessly like a dog.

"Tupla pinis na namba tri klostu bai kam na kain pipia man olsem yu bai yu lukautim ol olsem wanem – Two already and the third one is about to come and a trash like you, how are you going to look after them?

"Yupla olgeta lukim em, sem blong em – Everybody look at him, shame on him".

The man retaliated with provocations and the woman was blasting him with her diatribe as we left.

On the way my mind reflected on the fray and the sad reality dawned that I had witnessed an example of the disintegration and adulteration of customary nuptial principles.

The incident was a result of a classic domino effect triggered initially by the callous forces of westernisation.

In PNG, every ethnic group has its own traditional marriage customs, but the reign of peace, happiness and prosperity in marriage is a universal desire and Simbu and the rest of Papua New Guinea are no exception.

In Simbu society, there are four main elements in the marriage enterprise. Building a new home and making a new garden, bride price fixing and pride price payment, the marriage contract or holim bros bilong pik (holding pig's breast) and the initiation of the groom and bride into manhood and womanhood (independent living).

There are slight variations in the order of the events and the manner in which the rituals are conducted in each tribal group but, on the whole, the four elements are the core pillars of Simbu marriage customs.

In South Simbu, when a boy and a girl are in love and have agreed to get married, the first thing the boy's relatives do is build a new house and make a new garden for the couple-to-be.

And then they look forward to the call by the girl's relatives to set the bride price.

Word goes to the girl's relatives that the boy's people are

ready to marry their daughter.

The girl's relatives host a small feast and invite the boy's relatives to attend.

The purpose of the feast is threefold: to give official recognition to the relationship (betrothal); to unite the two families; and, the core one, to fix the bride price … the girl's relatives informing the boy's relatives the amount of bride price they want for their daughter.

In response the boy's relatives set a tentative time for when they will pay the bride price.

The bride price amount set for a girl depends on whether she is working, the status of the parents and other minor factors.

If the girl is working or comes from a high class family, the bride price is set high and vice versa.

When the appointed time for payment comes, the boy's relatives bring the bride price - mostly cash these days- to the girl's people.

In the old days they used shell money, stone axes and birds-of paradise feathers.

But today it is cold hard cash and, in some cases, a Toyota Land Cruiser is included, especially when the girl is highly educated and the boy's parents are business tycoons.

The wedding feast is reciprocal. It is the bride's people who host the first feast for the groom's people and this is when the holim bros bilong pik rite is conducted.

Later, the groom's people host the payback feast for the bride's people and this time the bride and groom are initiated into manhood and womanhood

The night before the bride's people host the wedding feast, the groom and his people congregate with the bride and her people in the bride's parents' house or the hausman and the elders and sages of both sides give skultok (edification). The skultok extends until dawn and covers all aspects of life from morality to survival, leadership, prosperity, charity, warfare, raising children and problem-solving interspersed with singing and tanim het (the turning head ritual), jokes and meals.

In the morning, the bride's people line up the pigs, cattle, and goats they intend to slaughter for the groom's people to inspect and agree - because they are going to match them in the payback feast.

Once a consensus is reached, the animals are slaughtered and cooked in big mumu pits.

While the mumu is cooking, all kinds of bilums, clothes and cooked and raw food that the bride's people gathered for the groom's people are given to them.

When the mumu is ready, the bride is dressed in the finest traditional regalia ready to be received by the groom's people.

The groom and some strong men and women are also dressed in traditional regalia and await the call for holim bros bilong pik.

As soon as the mumu is removed from the pits, word goes out to the groom that it's time for holim bros bilong pik. The groom and his friends sing and dance to the mumu place where the reception takes place.

The most colourful and exciting part of the ceremony is the receiving of the groom and bride by the respective sides.

Both sides mingle and dance in a warlike fashion and carry the bride and groom away before bringing them together for holim bros bilong pik, equivalent to the exchange of wedding rings in the western culture.

The exchange and eating of pig's breast then proceeds. The bride holds one breast and the groom holds another and they exchange them. The marriage is sealed.

The groom and the bride each take a bit of pork and carry the breast to their relatives to finish eating.

This is followed by brief, wise and heart-moving speeches by both sides (which also includes the timing of the return feast) before the bride is released to the groom's people amidst tears and dirges by the close relatives.

The groom's people take the bride, the meat and all the other stuff and return to their place.

The bride is taken to her new home and, in the days that follow, introduced to her new garden.

When the appointed time for the payback feast comes, the groom's people repay all the bilums, clothes, foods and animals that were slaughtered for them and sometimes even extra.

Before the woman's people go away with the food, the final ritual is conducted.

In front of the whole assembly, the woman is presented with a bilum (symbol of fertility), a spade (symbol of hard work), a female piglet (symbol of prosperity and wealth) and several kaukau vines (symbol of copiousness).

The man is presented with an axe (symbol of manhood, independence and hard work) and a sugar cane or banana seed of a very special kind (symbol of prosperity and leadership).

Making a new home and garden, skultok and initiating the bride and groom into womanhood and manhood are vital elements of the whole marriage venture for the Simbu people.

The couple is now well prepared to face the challenges of marriage and, few months after the bridal ceremonies, they are living an independent life.

Today, though, the unfeeling influences of western culture have disintegrated and adulterated marriage customs and some important elements of the vital nuptial rites are on the verge of dying out.

Skultok and manhood and womanhood initiations are forlorn rituals.

Holim bros bilong pik has been replaced by the exchange of rings in church. Traditional bilas is replaced by suits, ties and gowns.

For most marriages, the bride prices are not paid until some years after the women have children.

The couples don't have their own means of survival. They depend on their parents for shelter, food and clothes. Even after they have children, they continue to depend on their parents and become a liability.

When the bride price is paid, they have not gone through the skultok and other initiations and, as a result, don't know how to start a new and independent life.

All they know is sex and they think this is what marriage is about, but it's not. Only if they go through the skultok will they know that marriage is more than having sex and producing children.

When problems confront them they are confused and don't know how to handle them. Violence, desertion and marriage break ups are the ultimate consequences.

Some even wander into promiscuity and end up with HIV and AIDS.

Worse still, the wider permeation of pornography is influencing young people to adopt marriage practices before they are betrothed or wedded.

The whole matter is a national issue. It affects the entire nation. It affects the moral fabric of our society.

Society is continuously evolving and, if this kind of cultural disintegration continues, PNG is heading for a culture embedded in lost identity and moral decadence.

Perhaps one good way to preserve not only the nuptial but the other valuable and beneficial customs is to institutionalize them.

Each province could establish a cultural education institute where all the valuable and beneficial customs are documented in written and electronic form and are taught to the children in schools as part of their school lessons.

This is a complex and difficult issue that has no easy solution. The best each and every ethnic group can do is to regularly practice their customs. In this way custom is preserved; it is kept alive and passed on from generation to generation.

19

Eventually the Price for Parental Neglect Will be Paid

THE level of love and care we give to our children is the same level we will receive from them when we are sick or get old. If we give them the best according to what we have, we will get the same measure and even more from them.

Yesterday the news of the demise of Tabie reached me, and memories of human tragedy rekindled. He had been referred to Sir Joseph Nombri Memorial Hospital in Kundiawa from the Goroka Base Hospital before being sent back to Goroka.

Tabie was in his early sixties and it was some months ago that he was admitted to my ward for treatment of acute arthritis in both his legs.

Although he was able to walk with the support of crutches, he didn't have the strength to help himself with other daily chores.

My daughter Charlene (now doing grade 11 at Yauwe Secondary) helped him to fetch drinking water and to get his morning tea and dinner from the mess. She even did his laundry for him.

As days passed into weeks, we realised that none of his relatives were going to come to look after him. He lacked toiletry, so we helped him. We provided him with fruit and extra meals. Whatever we had we shared with him.

Sometimes Charlene would ask about his relatives and if they might come to look after him. Tabie said he didn't know.

"Do you have children?" she asked.

"Yes Bubu, I have many children. They are all grown-up and married. Two of them are in Port Moresby. One is teaching at Kilakila Secondary School and the other is operating a taxi service," Tabie replied proudly.

"Then why will none of them come to visit you? You need a guardian to look after you, bathe you, wash your clothes and get your meals from the mess. You are not strong enough to help yourself."

"Bubu, you are right. I don't know why they are not coming," he said with a tone of regret.

"Do they know you are here? Do you have their phone number?"

"They know I am here, Bubu but I don't know why they are not coming. I don't have their phone numbers."

"It's alright," Charlene assured him. "I will look after you and my dad."

Tabie stayed in the hospital for almost three months until being transferred back to Goroka. He was living with his latest wife, a widow, when he passed on a week ago.

All throughout his four months at Sir Joseph Nombri Memorial Hospital, only three visitors came to see him but they were not his family members. They were wantoks from the village (hauslain) who brought some food with them.

The first two who came were a couple. Charlene asked them why Tabie's children were not coming to look after him.

The man hesitantly said he didn't know why? The wife facing Charlene, with the back of her head to Tabie, twisted her nose.

I couldn't work out what the facial gesture meant.

Charlene, being an intuitive girl, grabbed the woman's hand and said, "Let's go and chew betel nut," and they went out.

About half an hour later they came back, their lips red with buai spittle.

When the couple left, Charlene bombarded Tabie with questions about the number of wives and children he had with his wife and how he parented the children. She had already learnt a lot about Tabie's life from the woman.

The truth then finally surfaced.

Tabie had been a handsome man in his young days and married one woman after the other. After the birth of his second child, he deserted the mother and the children and married a new wife.

As soon as the new wife had a child, he left them and married another one and he went on like that … a hit and run type.

He had nine children from his many wives.

He didn't look after any of his children. He didn't promote and support their physical, emotional, social and intellectual development, including their formal education … the usual parenting process from infancy to adulthood.

All the children were raised by their maternal grandparents or other people who put them through school and paid their school fees.

Biological fatherly love was something that all of Tabie's children missed most in their lives.

Tabie didn't realise he wouldn't be forever young, handsome and energetic. There would come a time when he would get old or sick and have to depend on his children for care and support.

When he got old and became ill, the children totally despised and neglected him.

When Charlene learnt of his promiscuous past and the neglect of his children, she stopped helping him. Tabie found life so hard so he was transferred back to Goroka.

Currently at Sir Joseph Nombri we have a patient paralysed by TB of the spine. He is in his fifties and was living a promiscuous life with no or little concern for his children.

His children would come and go. They didn't give a damn about his excrement and urine.

Many times he would yell and cry for help and the children would tell him to die. They told him straight that he never cared for them. They grew up in their mother's hands. Other guardians had pity on him and were helping him.

There are instances where children inflicted severe bodily harm on their biological mother or father because of parental negligence.

There are many Papua New Guineans like Tabie who follow the flesh without worrying about the consequences of their actions and end up paying the ultimate price.

Our children are precious gifts from God, our assets and heirs. They are the ones we will call upon in old age and in the time of sickness and other calamities.

It is inhumane and insane for people not to take care of their own children unless it is for medical, economic or other legitimate reasons.

20

Betel Nut is Here to Stay...so Let's Solve It

IT is most regrettable that people's lives, including very young lives, have to be destroyed because of one very divisive policy ... the banning of betel nut.

No amount of money will appease the pain suffered by the relatives of those three people or equate the value of those lives. No way.

When the NCD Governor, Powes Parkop first announced the policy in October 2013, I was one of those who opposed the idea in the Post Courier and PNG Attitude blog.

The essence of my argument was that betel nut sustains life, creates employment, creates wealth, has the potent to swing political power and banning it would create many problems.

I argued that there are families (whether they are Southern High Highlanders, Engans, Simbus or Hanuabadans) in Port Moresby city that survive on income from selling buai and to sever their only lifeline without providing them an alternative means of survival is akin to direct or indirect.

So far three people have died (one accidently and two murdered), all related to the betel nut ban. Apart from the dead, there are many others who have been physically assaulted by authorities who are engaged to enforce the ban. There has also been destruction of properties.

If Governor Parkop wants to pay compensation, he should also pay it for the mother who died at Gordons market. But even then, like I said, no amount of money will equate the value of those lives.

The employment power of betel nut cannot be underrated. It creates a chain of employment for many people. Buai farmers employ people who harvest and bag the nut. The wholesalers employ truck or boat owners to transport the nut they buy from the farmers to the wholesale market.

The retailers employ other truck or taxi owners to transport the nut they buy from the wholesalers to their employees (sellers) who are many and scattered in various locations. The employees then sell the nuts to the users.

If research was done on the number of people who are involved full time or casually in the betel nut business, we would be amazed to find that it is the single highest employer in PNG. This is one crop knows no regional, ethnic or cultural boundaries. Highlanders and coastals alike chew the nut and involve in its business.

Banning betel nut is like cutting off employment and so alternative employment must be created to put money in people's pocket so that there is food on the table. One cannot just sever people from their employment and let them go hungry. This will not work. People will still sell betel nut.

The economic importance of betel nut cannot be underrated. Buai has the potential to make people rich.

People have bought motor vehicles and dinghies and built permanent houses with buai money. They have paid bills and invested in their children's education.

Those who know the money making potential of betel nut put their lives on the line in search for it. Imagine Engans, Southern and Western Highlanders travelling as far as Oro and Sepik looking for it.

Think of the length and lawlessness along the Highlands Highway.

Many highlanders do not know how to swim. Several of them have drowned in rough seas while searching for betel nut. But this does not deter others. People still take the risks because there is money in it.

So banning betel nut has not and will not bring forth the intended outcome.

Although betel nut is a health hazard and a source of filth, it can exercise potent political influence.

Politically, Governor Parkop has dug his own political grave by his total buai ban policy because he seemed to forget that bulk of the population that gave him the mandate to govern are the ordinary people: taxi or PMV owners, low income earners and street vendors. In one way these people rely on buai money to take care of their daily needs or business activities. Banning betel nut is jeopardizing the lives of the very people who gave him mandate and Parkop can expect repercussions comes 2017.

If the Governor has not realised his mistake, he should by now and instead of banning buai, the NCDC must explore other means that are beneficial to all parties. If NCDC has run out of ideas then it should ask the public to contribute ideas and select the most amicable one and pay for it.

While it is not too late, he might like to consider the following option.

The NCDC should issue buai trading license and identification cards to traders, whether individuals or companies. The license should have terms and conditions spelt out clearly in Pidgin and Hiri Motu.

It should state the trading site, which may be at the main market or in front of one's residence or any other place mutually agreed to by the buai seller and the NCDC.

The NCDC must supply trash bins with the license number and location name printed on it and small plastic bags to the license holder free or for a small fee.

When people buy buai, they must also be given a plastic bag for the buai rinds and spittle and after they finish chewing, they must dump it in the trash bin. City trash collectors will then empty the bin and leave it behind for reuse.

When the plastic bags run out, the trader can get the NCDC to replenish them or buy them from the supermarket and pass the cost to the betel nut user by increasing the buai price.

Before closing for the day, the trader must clean up his or her designated spot.

City rangers for each electorate within the capital should check every licensed area to make sure the place is clean. Heavy penalties should be imposed on those who do not comply with the terms and conditions of the license.

Buai users who misbehave should be fined heavily to deter others from misbehaving.

Of course this has to be legitimized by NCDC to protect itself from law suits.

In this way no one is a loser, and very importantly, the responsibility of taking care of the rubbish is given back to the perpetrators in a regulated way. This will cut down the clean-up cost and other related problems like violence and killings that we have experienced.

The ball is now in Parkop's court. He must not forget that betel nut is here to stay no matter how hard he tries to get rid of it.

21

Shameless Exploitation of Disabled People by Opportunists

THE callous exploitation of disabled persons by able-bodied people as objects for economic gains through sham, coercion and duress is thriving in Papua New Guinea.

Since the PNG government's announcement of social security benefits for disabled people last year, disabled groups are springing up everywhere, most of them initiated by able-bodied opportunists.

These chancers mobilise and force disabled people to offer them money and pigs with promises of financial returns.

They force them to parade and even sleep on the streets to gain attention from the public and government.

There are designated days in the year when people with disability can commemorate and advocate for their rights in public instead of any odd time when they might become a public nuisance and cause disturbances.

Most disabled people are illiterate and vulnerable and able-bodied people are taking advantage of their ignorance and vulnerability to pursue their egoistic interests. Disabled people are human beings and they have all the rights that are enjoyed by able-bodied people. Their dignity, freedom and independence should be respected.

Article (3a) of the general principles of the Convention on the rights of Disabled Persons (UNCRDP) ratified by the PNG government in New York in 2013 states: "The principles of the present Convention shall include respect for inherent dignity, individual autonomy including the freedom to make one's own choices, and independence of persons".

Contrary to this, in PNG able-bodied people are mobilising and taking photos of disabled people and using them to gain financial from government agencies and donors under the pretext of helping the disabled.

They even claim to own disabled people. At a recent AusAID funded disabled people's workshop conducted by PNG National Assembly of Disabled People at the Catholic Resource Centre in Kundiawa, two able-bodied people (a male and female) who were self-inviters and supposed to be observers forced themselves into the discussions and, in a heated argument, each claimed to own 5000 disabled persons.

The scurrilous pair has been collecting money and pigs from disabled people promising them financial returns.

The disabled people that each claim to own are the same persons and they have become the meat in the sandwich in this tug of war.

How on earth in this 21st century can people claim to own other human beings? This is total insanity and amounts to slavery and disrespect for the rights of people with disabilities.

Disabled people are sick and tired of able-bodied people using them to gain money to build palaces and empires for themselves.

They may be disabled but they are capable of contributing meaningfully to the development of their community and country.

All they need are opportunities and empowerment so that they can become agents of change and make a difference in their community.

It is hoped that as people in authority and areas of influence become thoroughly informed of the needs and aspirations of people with disabilities, appropriate steps will be taken to create conducive environments and programs to assist them to live productive and meaningful lives.

[The woman mentioned above was summoned and convicted for stealing under false pretence and is serving her prison term at Barawagi when this story went to press. The man is struggling to make good his debts knowing very well that the law will be after his neck if he doesn't].

22

Provincial Disable Policy: the Way Forward for Disabled People

IN Papua New Guinea people with a disability are the most marginalized and neglected group and are suffering misery on daily basis.

Chauvinism and poverty are two killers of disabled people, particularly paraplegics and polio victims in our society.

Public ridicule and stigmatization are the worst forms of chauvinism creating social barriers that deter disabled people from exercising their freedom of movement and equal participation in community programs and activities.

People make mockery and call them names when they see them going around in public places. Hence in fear of being ridiculed and stigmatized, disabled people isolate themselves in the seclusion of their home environment.

The relatives are also in fear of public ridicule and stigma and lock them up at home when they go about doing their business. They don't allow them to take part in public meetings and community activities.

Worse still is keeping school age children at home and not allowing them to attend schooling.

The United Nations Convention on the rights of people with a disability states that "children with disabilities are not excluded from free and compulsory primary education or secondary education on the basis of disability" and that "persons with disabilities can access an inclusive, quality and free primary education and secondary education on an equal basis with others in the communities they live in". They should be given the necessary support to go to school.

Disabled people, particularly in rural areas are suffering from extreme poverty. Because of poor infrastructure and economic opportunities, compounded by the physical impediments, they are not be able to earn their own living. They depend heavily on relatives for financial support and general welfare.

Many times relatives regard them as liabilities and loathe, neglect and ill treat them.

As a result of all this, disabled people are psychologically self-defeated. They feel rejected by the family and the community. They feel dejected and useless. They feel that there is nothing better for them to live for. There is no meaning to life. All they see is hopelessness and bleak despondency.

Many lose their lives by calling it quits. For instance, there were eleven of us paraplegics living in Sir Joseph Nombri Memorial Hospital and seven have passed on. The main contributing factor to their demise was self-defeatism due to misery.

They did not fight for survival when they were faced with health problems like pressure sores, bladder and kidney stones and so forth. They simply gave up.

One of the deceased was a man around the age of 30. He had a kidney stone and the doctor told him to take care of his diet while on medication. He deliberately defied the doctor's advice and accelerated his own demise by drinking home brew and smoking marijuana heavily ... you could very well call it suicide.

Another one around the age of 35 years had typhoid, which is curable, but he totally refused medication. He plainly told the doctors that he wanted to die.

The doctors and nurses did everything they could to save his life but he refused it all and finally died. He called it quits.

The National disable policy spearheaded by Dame Carol Kidu during her tenure as the Minister for Community Development was rendered just a boneless piece of paper because there was no funding from the national government for its implementation. The policy is currently out of date and obsolete.

I understand it was under review last year. How far the review has progressed is anyone's guess.

The much publicized disabled people's welfare scheme announced by Peter O'Neill in 2013 was mere popularity bunkum. To date nothing has eventuated, while the minister responsible Louzaya Kouza is been busy battling her family affairs and local Morobe politics and doing virtually nothing for the nation under her ministry which includes people living with disabilities.

The best possible way forward in addressing the plight of disabled people is for each province to have its own provincial disability policy.

To my knowledge, Manus and Gulf are two provinces that have been moving in that direction under the guidance of the disabled policy experts within the National Disabled Board and other provinces should follow suit to address the plight of their disabled population.

Only through actively instrumenting policy will there be consistency in funding for disability-related programs and activities that will enable improvement in the misery of the disabled people. Otherwise the culture of ad hoc, one day shopping handouts or donations will continue and disabled people will continue to suffer chauvinism and poverty.

23

Out of Anguish Born an Invincible Foundation of Wonder

THE young man watched by his mother's hospital bed side as she succumbed to the nefarious disease TB before his very eyes.   The woman that bore him, nurtured and worked so hard as he grew up and was educated to be able to live an affluent modern lifestyle had passed on without fully realizing the benefits of all that she had invested in him.   The man was devastated. He was mentally torn into shreds. Worst of all, she had died of a disease according to medical science is curable. Why?

The young man pondered.

As he stood there anguished and perplexed, his tearful eyes caught sight of many other souls both young and old lying motionless in their beds either waiting for their time to come or recuperation. His heart went out to them. And he promised; "I will never leave this hospital".

Since then, the man has established an unbreakable bond with the hospital that found its most outstanding form in the foundation of a charity organisation of wonder that truly reflects the Simbu heart …'we hug when you expect a hand.' The organisation carries the motto 'Simbus helping Simbus – people helping people'.

Jimmy Drekore, the son of Barbina and Raphael Drekore of the Dinga number two tribe in the Sinasina Yongomugl District of the Simbu Province, Papua New Guinea, was born on September

15, 1976. He was the eldest in a family of six, with one brother and two sisters.

Jimmy grew up to school age under the watchful eyes of his mother Barbina and father Raphael. He attended Koge Primary School at the age of five. He did grade 1- 6 from 1982 to 1987. He completed grade 10 in 1991at Kondiu Rosary High School.

In 1992, Jimmy went down south to the Downlands College in Towoomba on the plateau west of Brisbane, Australia, on a three year study scholarship courtesy of AIDAB (Australian International Development Assistant Bureau).

At the end of the schooling, Jimmy returned to PNG and studied applied science at the Lae University of Technology from 1995 to 1998. He graduated with a bachelor degree in applied chemistry.

The following year, Jimmy joined Newcrest's gold mine at Lihir Island in the New Ireland Province of Papua New Guinea as an analytical chemist. After working for New Crest for 11 years, Jimmy resigned from the job in May of 2012 and since to date he spends full time on the charity that he founded.

In 2004, Jimmy's mother Barbina passed on at the Sir Joseph Nombri Memorial Hospital Kundiawa. Jimmy was devastated. It was very painful. Standing by the bedside of his dead mother in the hospital, Jimmy promised to never leave the hospital.

Two years later, the promise was manifested in a humanitarian organisation that has grown from strength to strength with its members comprising of Simbus of all creed and walks of life across the globe. And this humanitarian charity organisation is called Simbu Children Foundation (SCF).

Simbu Province in the central highlands of PNG is mountainous. Economic resources and opportunities are very limited. The annual average income for an average village family is less than thousand kina. That kind of money is not sufficient to meet all the financial needs of the family including medical expenses.

For a child with a heart problem is to travel to Port Moresby with the guardian or parent for the visiting specialist overseas doctors to operate on costs around K1500 to K2000 depending on the age of the child.

Most parents cannot afford this kind of money so the child has to die.

There are many such cases. The idea of SCF fills this vacuum addressing the social welfare needs of the poor. And Simbus in all works of life have enthusiastically volunteered when the idea of forming SCF was floated.

It initially started off as a family charity work. Straight after his mother's demise, Jimmy and his young wife Merrilyn Drekore embarked on a monthly protein diet supplement program by supplying milk, Milo, egg and chicken liver to the sick children in the paediatric ward which SCF has now taken over.

At the same time Jimmy floated the idea of forming the charity organisation to support the sick and disadvantaged children of Simbu with the aim of developing a healthy future for Simbu men and women among his Simbu work mates and colleagues. The response was heartening. Simbus in all works of life joined SCF and more are coming in each year.

Merrilyn, a secondary school teacher and a very understandable and cooperative wife, worked so hard along Jimmy to ensure that the idea become a reality. To date Merrilyn remains a force behind the successes of SCF.

By 2006 all formalities were in place and in 2008, the then Governor General Sir Paulias Matane officially launched the Foundation at a glittering occasion at Crown Plaza in Port Moresby.

Since then the organisation has grown from strength to strength in achieving its aim - helping the sick and disadvantaged children of Simbu.

Among its achievements are the purchase and delivery of a life-saving electric infant incubator from the United States of

America to the Genealogy ward, monthly supply of proteins for the malnourished children in the Paediatric Ward through a monthly protein diet supplement program, sponsoring of airline tickets and other logistics support for operation open heart patients and their guardians from Simbu to Port Moresby and return through the annual Brave Hearts sponsorship program and an annual Christmas barbecue and presents program for the sick children in the hospital.

The pinnacle of all the achievements is the funding of the research into osteomyelitis that I wrote featured in PNG Attitude blog and one of the Weekend Courier issues.

The research has the accreditation of Professor Peter Siba, the Director of the PNG Medical Research Institute (PNGIMR) in Goroka, Eastern Highlands Province. This means the research is worthy of having it published in any international medical journal.

The executives, members and benefactors of SCF are very happy because SCF in its very short history has gone into funding a scientific research project.

The next project SCF is currently embarking on is the construction of a mini hydro power generation for Irugl Care Centre at the foot of PNG's highest peak Mt. Wilhelm.

Irugl care centre now known as Mother of Life Center is a self-help care centre for orphans and disadvantaged children. The parents have either died of HIV & AIDS, accidents or other calamities or have broken up.

The centre was started by a Netherland national by the name of Martin Van der Palen in 2002. Martin came to Simbu as a lay missionary and married Agatha from Irugl. They lived and worked as lay missionaries in Simbu for 15 years before they moved to Netherlands. Agatha, while in Europe died. Her death wish was to build a charity home in her village Irugl where youths could be empowered by providing them the necessary support to attain some education and engage them in self-sustenance activities.

Martin has been raising funds in his home country and visiting Irugl once every year on tourist visa because the PNG government will not grant him citizenship on health reason. But the level of support has been diminishing to almost a self-support because of Martin's ill health.

The first product from the centre to enter a higher institution is Komba Bundo. He is in first year university at the Lae University of Technology.

Although Martin and Agatha have established a noble institution helping Papua New Guinean children, the centre is getting very little support from the state agencies.

SCF has been supporting the centre with food rations and second hand clothes. It identifies electricity as one of the important needs of the centre. Hence SCF is stepping in the way to help.

SCF volunteer engineers have already carried out site assessments and they are into the planning stage now. Once the planning is complete and the exact cost is established then, the next task is to find money to fund it.

The unique virtue of SCF is that it has been relying on its own fundraising and benevolent donations from Simbu elites mostly members/volunteers and Simbu men and women in business to execute its aims.

It has never knocked on the doors of donors, government agencies and politicians with a proposal since its inception. SCF stands on the principle that if someone sees and believes in what it is doing let them step forward with their support.

The principle has come of age in the year 2013 when a number of Simbu Members of Parliament stepped forward of their own accord with pledges of various amounts to support the work of SCF. The highest donation was K100, 000 from the Simbu Provincial Government under Governor Hon. Noah Kool. Second to that was K50, 000 from the Member for the Chuave Electorate,

Wera Mori. [Apart from the MPs, Kennedy Wemin of Melanesian Trustees Limited has been very supportive].

It has become obvious that the Simbu MPs have faith and trust in the kind of work that SCF has being doing.

It is hoped the National Planning Department will assist to fund the project.

[The proposal had been forwarded to the Department of National Planning and Monitoring in 2014 but to date nothing has eventuated.]

24

Kundiawa Town is Sitting on a Fiery Time Bomb

EVERY time I pass by the concrete ruin and look at the two brick walls standing sadly in solitude against the infinite assaults of sun, rain and wind at what is now known as Lodge Fire, I reflect on the risk of fire.

The remains are of what was once Simbu's most famous entertainment hub and premiere hotel, the Simbu Lodge.

One fateful day the property was razed to rubble by fire. At the time of the blaze, it was under the tenancy of some Asians.

My mind has been troubled in more recent times about what would happen if another fire occurs tomorrow?

The Simbu Lodge was built, owned and operated by Paul Mason, a son of one of the Australian planter and famous Coastwatcher of the same name based in Bougainville, until one fateful night in 1991 when it burned down.

Apart from Simbu Lodge, Paul operated shops but moved out of Simbu some years after the fire.

According to Mathias Miugle, a former employee and currently chef of Sir Joseph Nombri Memorial Hospital, the fire started in the kitchen at around 11pm on a Saturday night.

There was a power blackout and it seems the chef, Philip Kawale, forgot to switch off the deep fryer.

When the power came back after some time later, the oil in the fryer heated to the extreme and ignited. The flames leapt to the gas cylinders which became fiery missiles and were projected everywhere.

The fire spread to other parts of the building so fast that guests and workers fled for their lives with little or no time to gather up their personal belongings. Everything went up in flames.

The people stood afar and watched in fright. Only looters and opportunists risked their lives and grabbed whatever they could lay their hands on.

There was nothing anyone could do to stop the fire because of the enormous flames and the intense heat.

There was no fire-fighting service available back then – there still isn't one today.

By morning, the entire structure had been reduced to rubble. The once beautiful hub of leisure and enjoyment was turned into an ugly mess of corrugated iron and metal frames.

To date only remnants of the concrete slab and the brick walls remain. As time passes and memory erodes, people tend to forget the Simbu's most destructive fire in history. But the seriousness of the incident and the impact of it should not be underrated.

In hours, the fire destroyed an investment worth millions of kina. As a result, many people were put on to the streets without job. The provincial government lost one of its most reliable sources of internal revenue.

The question on my mind for a long time is how could we control a fire tomorrow? Without fire services, sadly the answer to that question is, we couldn't at all.

Kundiawa town is a fire time bomb. The matchbox-shaped main shopping centre ... Four Corner Town as is popularly known is of extreme fire risk.

Most of the buildings were constructed in the 60s and early 70s and are worn, torn and forlorn due to old age and lack of maintenance. Walls and ceilings are falling apart. Electrical wiring is exposed.

One small electrical spark or flame in a kitchen could set ablaze the entire commercial centre. There could be many casualties.

The Kondom Agaundo Building, the old hospital that currently houses the education division and most of the teachers' houses and classrooms at Kundiawa Lutheran Day Secondary School are all in deteriorated state.

TNA Company has erected a couple of modern structures that could resist and delay the spread of fire but they are not totally immune.

Most of the shops do not have fire extinguishers. When they do, they are mostly old, unmaintained and non-functional.

Kundiawa Town is famous for water shortages and water supply disruptions initiated by land owners negating the limited number of fire hydrants in town.

The PNG Fire Service is one of the worst funded and poorly equipped government agencies. It does not have the capacity to expand its service to centres like Kundiawa.

Simbu is not the only province at fire risk. More than half the provinces in PNG are in the same boat.

About a year after I got this story published on PNG Attitude blog, a number of shops in Goroka were razed to ashes. The ill equipped fire fighters located only a few meters away could not contain the fire. Which town will be the next?

With the LNG income flowing in, fire-fighting service is one area that the government should improve and expand on.

25

The Contradictions Implicit in Judging Personality

IN my walk of life I come across people who sometimes confuse me with their personality, particularly those who have crossed over from the dark side.

Many times I have met up with this guy who once wilfully murdered a man, was imprisoned, served his time, got his freedom back, married a beautiful wife, joined the police force as a reservist and is currently one of the top officers.

Every time I meet him, I am confounded as to what kind of personality tag to confer on him.

And there is this public servant who was accused of stealing state funds while he was a district manager. He appeared in court, was found guilty and sentenced to six months imprisonment with hard labour.

He served his time, came out, somehow got back into the public service and is now occupying one of the senior positions in his department. I hear that he is considered one of the most hard working and honest officers.

Each time I see him on the road in his government white Toyota Land Cruiser, I feel muddled as to what kind of personality he might have.

Then there is this other guy who was accused of raping a teenager. He was arrested, appeared in court and pleaded guilty.

He was sentenced to two and half year imprisonment with hard labour.

While in prison, he joined a Christian denomination and was converted. Straight after he got out of prison, he attended bible college and became a pastor of the church, preaching the word of God.

Whenever I see him, I am confused as to what kind of personality he really has.

Another case. A politician who was accused of misappropriation. He appeared in court and was found guilty. He paid the penalty imposed on him and sometime later was awarded an ambassadorial post in a prestigious foreign mission.

Every time I read about him, I get myself confused about his personality.

There are many others, not only men but women in this society, who have gone through a similar experience in life.

Maybe I am suffering from some sort of vacillation complex which bewilders me when trying to confer a personality tag to each of them.

I guess I'll leave it up to others.

26

Is It Just Us - or Is the Whole World Stupid?

THERE are some things that human beings - to be specific Papua New Guineans - do that, when I consider them critically, I find to be so absurd as to wonder whether they have brains.

There was this mother selling taro nicely creamed in coconut oil with spring onion and garlic puree. You could smell it from afar.

Her grown-up girl came back from school and she was hungry. The mother gave her one kina from the money she had earned from the sale of the taro and told her to buy a bun known as dry scone.

The girl grinned and walked to the nearest bun seller, got herself a dry scone and sated her hunger while other people bought taro from her mother for one kina and ate it with coconut milk and garlic and onion soup served on plate. A delicious and healthy snack.

Another time I saw a woman selling oranges at our small market at the hospital's front gate for K1 and 50t. Her little kid came crying to her for something. Instead of giving the child an orange, the mother gave her a kina and told the kid to buy a bottle of Tang.

The kid ran to the Tang seller and, wearing a broad smile, came back carrying a bottle of the sugary beverage.

There is a fisherman from Wara Simbu who catches trout in the river. Each time he catches a big one, he sells it. With the money, he buys lamb flaps, an animal product classified as health hazard and unfit for human consumption in Australia and New Zealand. There it's processed into animal feed but it also floods PNG supermarkets because dogs and Simbu fishermen likes it.

I see many coastal people doing the same thing. They toil in the rough seas, fighting the wind, rain and sun, to catch fish to sell them at the market.

After they sell everything, they buy lamb flaps and tinned fish full of additives and little quantity and take them home to eat.

A mother and daughter sold English potatoes at the main market. In the evening they bought a packet of rice to take home. Before catching a PMV, they were in one of the Chinese fast food places eating potato chips.

Whenever I think about these things, it makes me wonder which part of their body these people use for thinking. It can't be their brains.

And I wonder whether there are people like them in Australia, New Zealand and other countries or do we only have them in Papua New Guinea.

27

Can I Thank You for Your Human Compassion?

An unexpected telephone call one early morning from Pastor Robin Lillicrapp from Brisbane, Australia, set the ball rolling and before I knew it I was the proud owner of a special air mattress, custom built wheel chair and an array of special vitamins and supplements designed to get me back to normal health. This is my thank you message that was published on PNG Attitude blog. The article received applauds from many commentators. One of them was Russell Soaba, the author of 'Wanpis' and senior lecturer in language and literature, UPNG. Russell wrote, "A beautiful story. It beats all genres of writing in Papua New Guinea."

I CANNOT find the right words to express my heart's gratitude for all my friends in Australia and Papua New Guinea who have poured out their hearts so compassionately to support and ease my physical condition … only silent tears say it all.

An unexpected telephone call one early morning from Australia set the ball rolling and before I knew it I was the proud owner of a special air mattress, custom built wheel chair and an array of special vitamins and supplements designed to get me back to normal health.

In my life as a paraplegic I have been confronted with all kinds of challenges, both physical and spiritual, and some of them are very painful but I don't whine and cry. I have always asked myself: would whining and crying help me? And I find that they don't. They only weaken my spirit and my strength and make my condition worse. So I have developed an iron-hearted approach to the challenges that come my way. But I now realise that in every iron heart there is a softer part and, when you touch that, it can melt and the brooks of heaven burst forth.   For the past few days I have been in mourning. The compassion that has been shown by my family of writers and readers in Papua New Guinea and Australia, and even as far as Nairobi in Kenya and Sioux Lookout in Canada, to ensure that my life not only continues but is changed for the better has been so overwhelming that I have been moved to tears.

These very humane friends have touched my heart so much that every time I tried to write this thank you note, tears blurred my vision and I had to lay it off several times. Being a paraplegic and unemployed has made life for me very challenging. Many times, especially in the first two years of my disability, I prayed to the Lord God, the author of my life, to simply take my life away.

I refused to face the world in the completely different perspective of a man in a wheelchair. The thoughts about the numerous impediments I would confront daily were a nightmare. I just wanted to go away and be at peace in heaven. But God did not take away my life. He has His own plan for my life and I have seen His hands many times in many ways.

The accident happened in February 1999 in Goroka. I was hospitalised in Goroka for about two months before obtaining a voluntary discharge because of the very poor service.

I spent the rest of the year in Goroka setting up a home for my children with my final entitlement from the public service, which wasn't much. In February 2000, I came to the Sir Joseph Nombri Memorial Hospital in Kundiawa for further treatment.

In early 2001, spinal fixation surgery was attempted but failed because of a secondary complication.

In February 2000, I came to the Sir Joseph Nombri Memorial Hospital in Kundiawa for further treatment.

While the operation was in progress, my right lung collapsed. My right diaphragm had been cut open from close to the navel right around to the spine. When my right lung was exposed, it could not cope and collapsed.

Although my whole body was numb as a result of the anaesthetic, my mind was still functioning at a certain degree of consciousness and I felt that my breath was going to stop at any moment.

The doctors confirmed later that I told them my breath was going to stop - and I passed out. The doctors saw the lung had completely stopped working, did what they could to resuscitate it and immediately stitched it up. They did not do the spinal fixation.

When I regained consciousness, I found myself in the surgical ward with infusion tubes, cannulas and drainage pipes all over my body. It was tormenting.

While I was recuperating from the failed surgery, I developed severe pressure sores. These were caused mainly because I had to lie still in one position for some days. The hardness of the ordinary mattress also contributed. My water mattress was too big for the hospital bed so I had left it back home in Goroka where it was stolen.

Several times I went under the blade of the surgeon's knife for the removal of the necrotic tissue. There was also skin grafting.

There are many scars around my buttocks and hips – the residual marks of pressure sores and surgeons' blades.

Sometime later my surgeon and priest, Dr Jan Jaworski from Poland, got me a second-hand water bed, which was very helpful. All the sores healed. I was able to move around in my wheelchair, be independent and do the things I wanted to, including writing stories and poems. But to get the writing published was hard.

Then in 2011, Jimmy Drekore introduced me to *PNG Attitude* and The Crocodile Prize. Since then I have been writing and sharing my thoughts with my family of writers and readers from Papua New Guinea and Australia on *PNG Attitude* and through the annual Crocodile Prize Anthology.

My current condition developed from a mishap that occurred on my return from attending the 2012 writers' workshop and Crocodile Prize award ceremony at the Australian High Commission in Port Moresby in September.

When I arrived in Goroka, my daughter Cheryl, who was supposed to be waiting for me at the airport, was stranded in Kundiawa. She was unable to catch a bus. Worse than that, my mobile phone battery had gone dead ... total communication blackout. I had not charged it the night before.

I waited at the Goroka airport for two hours and still there was no sign of Cheryl. I couldn't wait any longer because it was getting late. I offered some tips to a group of boys and they assisted me to the bus stop and into a bus that was crammed full.

There were only three seats remaining and I sat in the one close to the doorway. There was plenty of cargo and it was very awkward for me but I refused to complain. In a way I had no choice.

On the way to Kundiawa, my right tibia fractured below the kneecap. The road condition was very poor, riddled with crater size potholes. As the bus maneuvered its way around them, I was tossed about and in one of those movements I must have hit something that broke my leg.

I didn't know, and I didn't feel anything, until two days later when my leg became severely swollen. Of course I suspected something was wrong. I went for an x-ray and the picture revealed the fracture.

A back slab was wedged around my ankle for 12 weeks and it severely impeded my mobility in bed.

More woe, my second-hand water bed developed holes and was rendered useless. Pressure sores started to develop. Although my leg was healed, the pressure sore under my left buttock got worse.

I went under the doctor's blade and the necrotic tissues were removed but the sores had not improved because of the hard mattress I was using, and other reasons as well. I was confined to bed for more than a year.

I go out once in a while to get natural vitamin D from the sun because I was becoming a carrot. Otherwise I stayed in bed all the time and did all my writing lying on my back.

I have never before discussed publicly the previous accident or the latest mishap, nor the consequent experiences and problems that I endured – except with other people like my family members and Jimmy Drekore, who is like a son to me.

When some of my friends asked me to write about it, I bluntly refused. I have been keeping everything to myself and battling on silently.

This is the first time I am sharing it all openly and I really feel obliged to do so in appreciation of the overwhelming support rendered to me by some beautiful and kind-hearted people.

Thank you so much for your compassion and benevolent support. The heart you have shown is awesomely inspirational and elating.

I will certainly get well and continue to share with you pieces of my mind in *PNG Attitude*.

The loving grace of the Lord shall be with you all.

28

Dreams and Ambitions Chattered at Their Prime

I have decided to include this autobiography as an afterthought. Often when we read a book, we would like to know the brain (author) behind it. Hence this brief autobiography is to give the reader a glimpse of the author.

AN isolated and shattered journey is probably the best way to describe my life.

As a child, I was rarely allowed to go out to public gatherings on my own or go out and play with other children.

My parents would allow other children to come to my home and play with me. Whenever I sneaked out, I had to return early. If I didn't, they would look for me. If it was my father, a slab was the pay.

Well, it is natural for parents to have concern for their children but it was a bit too much on the part of my parents, particularly my father. Even when I was old enough, he was exercising control over my life until I went to school.

I often argued with him why he didn't give me the freedom that other village children enjoyed. Dad never explained why. I was to find out at a later stage.

My grandfather Duma Sina was the paramount chief. The colonial administration appointed him to become boss-boi (headman or supervisor). He came to be known as Duma Bospe in my Yui dialect.

He worked extensively with the Kiaps in the construction of roads, bridges and outposts, undertaking censuses and other tasks in my area. One of the road constructions he was involved with was the Gumine-Kundiawa highway.

Although grandpa was the paramount chief, he never practiced polygamy. He had a concubine. His brother died at a very young age leaving behind his wife with two young children, a boy and a girl. Grandpa took them under his wing and looked after them. They become part of the Duma family.

Grandpa lived to very old age and died peacefully in his sleep in 1984.

My father was the last born in a family of two males and two females. Although he was the last born, he inherited the chieftainship of his father.

He was appointed Tultul (deputy head man) by the colonial administration. He worked with grandfather and helped the Kiaps in their work. He still carries the title Tultul today.

I was born to become the first and the last child of Nii-Kaupa Niigrus (Nicholas) Duma and Erkina Tinegiring in the Sina-Duma lineage of the Moiwo-Buba clan of Yui-Yobai, Salt LLG, Karimui Nomane District of the Simbu Province, Papua New Guinea.

From the stories I learnt, my mother had almost died of delivery complications and haemorrhage while delivering me in the kunai thatched family home at Mountain Yobai.

She passed out from excessive bleeding and the local midwives thought she was dying. They called my father and he assembled the traditional medicinal men who then administered all the traditional medication they knew and they saved my mother's life. As a result, Mum and Dad vowed not to have another child.

True to their vow, they did not give me a brother or sister until mum passed on in 1992 of illness. Dad is still rolling his favourite tobacco and puffing it away at Mountain Yobai, the place that I have dearly missed so much.

Father knew he would not be having another child and I became the apple of his eye. He took great care of me, the disposition I took it wrongly as excessive restriction and isolation.

My educational life was tough but I managed to make it through.

In 1973, I attended Grade 1 at the age of ten at Diani Primary School, 3 kilometres from home. I had to walk to school and back every day for six years.

Kaukau roasted in the ashes of fire and cold water had been my lunch for each of those gruesome years.

The school was newly established and I was one of the pioneers. We had to do a lot of physical work like constructing the playing field, building classrooms and teachers' houses with bush materials.

With my totally illiterate background, classroom lessons were new and difficult. But as time progressed, I got the hang of it and passed the Grade 6 examinations.

I progressed to Yauwe Moses Secondary, then Chuave Provincial High School, more than 100 kilometres away from home.

Mark Rosen, an Englishman and a veteran educationist, was the headmaster for the four years.

Apart from the nationals, I was privileged to have been taught by expatriate teachers Alfred Kaethler from Canada and Diane Smart from Great Britain who then married each other and Barry Bollinger from Australia who married to a Simbu woman.

Diane was my English and guidance teacher. She was the one who encouraged me to read a lot of books.

Very strict school regulations and discipline at Chuave helped to shape and mold my general behaviour and approach to schooling.

Apart from school work, I was also involved in sports. Soccer and volley ball were my favourites. Rugby league was banned in schools during my time.

At weekends, I went swimming with my friends at Mai River or scaling mountains including Mt Elimbari.

The hardest part of high school was finding enough school fees. My parents were typical subsistence farmers. But they sold pigs and paid my school fees.

Many times foods were insufficient and I would go hungry. Eventually I learnt to accept hunger as a normal part of high school life.

Towards the end of the Grade 10 academic year in 1982, I wanted to go on to national high school to do Grades 11 and 12. But Diane wanted me to go direct to the University of Papua New Guinea and attend the one year matriculation course.

I disagreed but, after a long discussion, she eventually convinced me that I could do it. I heeded her counsel and I made it to UPNG the following year.

Again it was tough but I managed to get through to full matriculation. I could go into any faculty. I chose to take up arts majoring in economics.

The freedom that I had been deprived of for all those years I found at UPNG. There was total freedom. I was the boss of my own life. I could spend the day in class or join my wantoks and have beer parties at Two-Mile Hill or Six-Mile Settlement and no one would question me or punish me.

But I had to get my priorities right. So I put my studies first, rugby league second and going out with my wantoks third. My life at UPNG revolved mainly around these three activities.

I also became involved in writing poems and in poetry recitals as past-time activities. I was a founding member of the PNG Writers Union which became defunct after few publications.

The five years of university student life came to an end in 1987. Fifteen consecutive years of student life; I felt, was too much.

With a bachelor's degree in economics in hand, my desire to find a job and earn money became strong.

My first choice was PNG Defence Force.

For three Christmas breaks, I had worked for the PNGDF in the registry and finance sections at Murray Barracks and I really enjoyed the environment there. I had been given a room at the single quarters rent-free and three meals a day for only five kina a fortnight at the privates' mess.

I had a discussion with the human resources manager on the prospect of joining PNGDF and he promised me that I would start at the rank of Captain in the Policy and Planning Division. From there I could work my way up to Brigadier General. I fell for it.

When I sought my father's consent, he disagreed outright. He gave me no room for negotiation. My dream of priding myself with three golden peeps shinning on my shoulders was shattered.

My next career choice was banking. I approached Westpac and Rural Development banks. My enquiry with the Rural Development Bank turned out an interview. I was told that I could commence work the next day. I started working for money the very next day at the bank's head office at Waigani. That was in February 1988.

I worked for the Rural Development Bank, now National Development Bank in various positions spanning 11 years. I was ambitious in my approach to work and climbed up the ranks so fast and that enabled me to travel and work in places like Rabaul, Kimbe, Bialla, Namatanai, Manus and Kainantu. I was more or less a trouble shooter deployed to fix, diffuse and soothe problems.

My first daughter Cheryl was born at Nonga Base Hospital in Rabaul. My second daughter Maggie was born at Bialla Health Centre in the West New Britain Province and the third girl Charlene was born at Manus Hospital in the Manus Province.

My experiences in Manus were most memorable. My family and I had lovely times picnicking at the white sandy Salame beach or boating up the Kari River. I would go fishing in the crystal blue waters of Andra and hunting for cuscus up in the highlands of Tingou. There would be no intrusion. It was free and peaceful.

My last destination of work was Goroka and that was where I had an accident that left me paralysed. My highly successful career ended. My dreams and ambitions were shattered at the very prime of my career and life.

The accident happened in February 1999. After spending one year in Goroka, I came to Kundiawa General Hospital.

After a spinal fixation attempt failed, I was located in the Isolation ward and I have been living there ever since.

So many things have happened since the accident and most have been for worst and not for better. There were times that I smelled death, and thank God for not taking my life away.

While living in the hospital, I published my first novel Paradise in Peril in 2005. It was an amateur's work at its best. However, surprisingly there was high demand for it.

I wanted to publish a second edition but I couldn't find a cheaper publisher until I got connected to Keith Jackson's PNG Attitude blog, the home of the Crocodile Literature Competition, courtesy of Jimmy Drekore. And that's where the door has opened up for me.

Phil Fitzpatrick of Pukpuk Publishing was instrumental in assisting me to get the abridged copy of Paradise in Peril published on Amazon e-Books in May 2013 under a new title *Fitman, Raitman & Cooks: Paradise in Peril*. My gratitude goes to Phil for his tireless and invaluable assistance.

Thanks to Keith for providing the flat form and mentoring and promoting Papua New Guinean writers and literature. I have been privileged to have my writings published in *PNG Attitude*.

I would like to take this opportunity to encourage Papua New Guineans to write. In PNG, there is a wealth of things to write about. We have exotic cultures, diverse flora and fauna, so many unrecorded heritages and socio-political history to write about. Become one of those immortal souls that live beyond the grave.